Tao:
The Way of God

by Master Waysun Liao

Copyright ©2010 Waysun Liao
Taichi Tao Productions
433 South Blvd., Oak Park, IL 60302
www.taichitaocenter.com

ISBN 978 0 9765454 4 6

All Rights Reserved
Nothing in this book may be reproduced
or reprinted in any form or by any means,
Including electronic or mechanical, photocopying or
recording, without the express permission of the publisher.

Table of Contents

Introduction	9

PART ONE: What is God?

A Magical Pastry Chef?	17
Everything is Made from One Substance	18
The Whole Universe is Alive	21
Emptiness is not Empty	24
Lao Tzu's Power of Weak and Small	33
The One Universal Energy is Intelligent	29
Lao Tzu Describes What God is Like	33
God's Power to Materialize	38
God is One Piece	40

PART TWO: The Spiritual Dimension

The Spiritual Dimension	45
All Beings Move Out From and Return to the Center	49
Different Layers and Levels of Energy	54
Many Spiritual Levels – Many "gods"	61
So-Called "Good" Energy and "Bad" Energy	64
We are Made from Recycled Energy	69

PART THREE: Who Are We?

We are Limited by False Understanding	77
Our Broken Connection to God	79
Humans Keep Trying to Create Heaven	82
The World Keeps You Busy and Keeps You from God	87
The Dead Treat Everything as if it were Dead	90
Profit Versus Passion: How Good Systems Get Hijacked	94
Government and the Need for Freedom	99
Why Laws and Morals Can't Solve the Problem	108
Religion's Big Mistake	115
We are All Connected	119
God is a Force of Balance	124
It's Easy to Worship the Wrong God	131

PART FOUR: Restoring Our Connection to God

Moving Meditation is Our Main Tool	137
We are Like Cell Phones	138
We Must Learn How to Return to God	141
The Real Goal of Taichi	143
Taichi is Like a Refining Oven	147
The Goal of Our Transformation	151
Establishing Your Lifestyle	155
Taichi Meditation and Sincerity	158
Our Common Sense Cannot Comprehend	160

Life Energy: Restoring the Power of the Single Cell	164
Our Body, Life Energy and Spirit are All Important	168
Birth, Illness, Aging and Death	170
The Highest Achievement	175
The Importance of Te	179
Go to Te Instead of Thinking	183
The Way Back to God is by Reduction	187
The Most Powerful Person	192
Go to God with No Strings Attached	198
Prayer is Like Launching a Rocket	203
Stop Negative Thinking Early and Quickly	205
Kindness Means Don't Judge	209
Remember Not to Worship the Wrong God	215
Stay Connected – Do Not Rely on Your Own Power	219
The Five Senses can Trick You	228
Our Fakeness can be Used to Mislead Us	237
Free Will Means Freedom from Evil	243
Escape from Wrong Thinking	246
Acceptance, Forgiveness and Ignoring Evil	251
Nothing Between You and God	256

PART FIVE: The Grand Tao

Restoring Ourselves – Restoring the World	267
The Rule of Balance	272

Introduction

The word "Tao" means the "Way." The way of what? The way to where?

Tao, in its original meaning, refers to God and the way God works. This "way God works" is also called "Dao," "Do," "Shin Do," depending on which area of Asia you travel, or which translations of old wisdom you read. For convenience, we will use the spelling T-A-O (pronounced *"Dow"*) to mean this ultimate original God, and the way in which this ultimate God's power unfolds.

The teachings contained in this book may seem new, even to those who have read many other books on Tao. That's because from its very beginning, Tao's core teaching had no real written record. Tao's core wisdom could only be found in the verbal transmission from master to disciple given "mouth to ear." Nevertheless, volumes of Tao literature exist because some people who touched this teaching enthusiastically tried to put it down into words. In many texts, they wrote what they knew in secret code so that the knowledge wouldn't fall into the hands of the wrong person. This makes most old writings about Tao very confusing for even the most sincere seeker.

The real teaching of Tao often took painstaking years of study in a temple, with a master patiently working with each disciple. The disciple would enter the temple as a monk after walking away from his or her regular life and giving up all ties to the outside world. Once inside the temple, the disciple's entire life would be devoted to study and practice. As they worked side-by-side in the temple gardens, the master might repeat the old wisdom and the old stories, answering questions and correcting the monks' misunderstandings. The disciples took each teaching to heart, and were expected to practice meditation and change their very nature so that they could better hear and understand their master's teaching. It was a demanding life with many trials and lessons, and many monks didn't make it and would quit. Yet a few monks would persevere and become masters for the next generation of those seeking the Tao. In this way, the temple tradition carried on for thousands of years.

Unfortunately, most people today do not have the benefit of temple life. Most of those old masters who knew how to teach about Tao as the "Way of God" died long ago. People are left muddling around on their own, sifting through translations of dusty old scrolls, or studying the interpretations and well-meaning speculations of scholars and would-be spiritual guides.

More complicated than this, when we study about Tao, we are using our limited human logic to try to comprehend God. This is an impossible proposition! We are no better off at this than fish trying to comprehend the universe that lies outside of the marine world. The only way to do this is to transform from a fish into a monkey and crawl out of the water to have a look around.

Likewise, we need to transform ourselves and rise to a different nature of being in order to truly understand God. This need is part of the message of Tao wisdom. But over the years, the instructions on how to make that transformation were hidden and revealed to only an exclusive few.

The time has come to give the teaching of Tao back to the world in as plain and simple language as possible. Why? Human beings have brought themselves to a crossroads. Our human civilization has changed beyond what we could have ever imagined even a short century ago. We have experienced more change to the way human beings live and what human beings know in the last one hundred years, than over the last several thousand years put together.

Consider this: How many thousands of years did human beings live much the same way? We had farms, close families, feudal kingdoms of one kind or another, we rode horses or walked for our transportation, and our means of communication were limited. We lived pretty much the same way for many centuries.

Then, all of a sudden, the twentieth century brought profound changes to every part of human life. The airplane, the telephone, modern medicine, the computer, television and radio, modern warfare, space travel, the automobile...The list goes on and continues to grow. One hundred years is a very short time for our human species to absorb so much change.

Add on top of this the incredible growth in numbers of our world population. We've expanded from one billion to 6.7 billion people on this planet in a very brief time.

The changes to our technology, and the impact of the sheer number of people on the planet, bring not only breathtaking advancements, but also create the risk that we could be facing any number of disasters. You do not need a crystal ball, an Ivy League degree, or even a Taoist master's insight to see that our world is standing at the edge of a dangerous cliff.

If we do not find a way to change our course, we could face any of several risks for catastrophe: whether our population exhausts or destroys our planet's fresh water supply, or we cannot provide enough food for everyone, or a critical part of our ecosystem collapses, or our political divisions result in man-made destruction through warfare, terrorism and the scramble for dwindling resources.

It is because of the dangerous disasters we now face, that this is the precise time the message of Tao needs to be available to all. But the good news is that it now can be available to all. Thanks to our technological advancements, we now have easy access to books, the Internet, DVDs, digital technology and jet travel, making it possible for people from all over the world and from all walks of life to avail themselves of this teaching. Our new technology allows us to preserve and pass on these old teachings via a virtual temple. Now everyone can learn the teachings and practice of the ancient Tao masters. You don't have to leave home and wander around to find a temple and a master. They can now come to you! It is truly good news that this message can now be accessed by virtually anybody around the world, because this message is needed now more than ever before.

With this book in hand, you have an invitation to enter into your own Tao journey. On that journey you will discover answers on how to restore harmony and healing for yourself and for mankind. When you understand Tao as the way God works, then you will have a roadmap showing you the way back to God.

Throughout this book, there will be quotes from the *Tao Te Ching*, written by Lao Tzu. For those of you unfamiliar with this famous work, it is the record of an old master in ancient China who was one of the first to use the term "Tao" to describe the way of God. Next to the Holy Bible, the *Tao Te Ching* is the most enduring, most widely translated and analyzed piece of literature in recorded history.

Lao Tzu did not invent Tao wisdom, but he was one of the first to write about it in a powerful and concise way. The words of the *Tao Te Ching* seem mysterious and hard to understand for many readers. But once you learn more about the way of God, Lao Tzu's words will become clearer to you. I often tell my students to read and re-read the *Tao Te Ching* 10,000 times if necessary. Even if you do not understand it, there is something deep inside of you that will understand.

It's important to note that what Lao Tzu writes about in the *Tao Te Ching* is not necessarily the same thing as today's "Taoism." The religion called "Taoism" combined Lao Tzu's teaching with other spiritual teachings that were popular in the centuries after Lao Tzu's death. These were mixed with local superstitions and even forms of sorcery in some instances, to create many different and complicated branches of today's "Taoism." Some Taoist sects even turned Lao Tzu himself into a "god," although nowhere does Lao Tzu make such claims about himself.

To truly understand Tao as the way of God, put aside what you know and what you've heard about "Taoism" for now. In fact, putting aside everything you think you know is the very best way to approach Tao.

PART ONE:
What Is God?

A Magical Pastry Chef?

When people wonder about God, they ask themselves: "How can God be all-powerful and everywhere at the same time?" or "How did God create the whole universe out of nothing?" These seem like impossible propositions. Such ideas are so hard for our human minds to grasp, but let's try anyway.

Let's pretend God is like a magical pastry chef. When we sneak into his kitchen, we observe that with only two substances, flour and water, this magical pastry chef can simply say, "Let there be cake!" All of a sudden, there is a cake. He says, "Let there be croissants!" and there are croissants. "Let there be cookies!" and a vast array of cookies appear before our eyes. Actually, he doesn't even need to speak. All he needs to do is think "crackers," and a plate of crackers magically appears.

Now all our magic pastry chef does is think "Cake!" and the flour and water instantly respond to form a cake. Why? How?

Our magic pastry chef, God, can perform such instant miracles because in addition to being the intelligent and skillful master baker, God himself is also the substance of the flour and water. Because the flour and water are perfectly connected with, and one in the same as his intelligence, they instantly respond to his will and intelligence.

It seems like a silly analogy, and in the course of this book we will talk more about this super-power ability of God to materialize anything instantly. However, let's take some time to explore more about God so that we can understand how our universe works and how this "magic pastry chef" analogy may not be so silly after all.

Everything is Made From One Substance

Everything, everywhere, is made up of one substance—one universal energy. Everything we see and experience—you, me, plants, animals, galaxies, the sky, the sun—all spring from this one same universal source energy. This one energy, this one substance, comes from, and is, God.

You may ask, "How can that be? All of these things in our universe are so different?" Yes, everything appears to be very different. For example, you might think the chair you are sitting in is very different from the air you are breathing. But they are not as different as they seem. What we call solid matter and what we call empty space are both made from the same "stuff."

The only difference between what we call space and what we call matter is whether this one universal energy, this "stuff," is traveling fast or slow. In our physical world, everything that is solid and material—like our chair—is made from this one energy moving very slowly. On the other hand, what we call space or emptiness, things we can't really see or touch, is this same energy moving very fast.

This one energy moving fast or slow is also moving in one of two directions: inward or outward. Think about it. If everything flies in toward one center, it slows down and compresses to become a particle. These particles, in turn, form objects like your chair. If everything flies apart and outward from the center, it disperses into space – like the thin air you are breathing.

The ancient Tao masters called the inward and outward forces of how energy moves "Yin" and "Yang." They said that when God or "Tao" created the universe, it first divided into "Yin" and "Yang." Everything we see, everything around us, has a force pulling inward and a force pushing outward. These two forces are the backbone of everything God created in this universe. Everything has "Yin" and "Yang."

If you think about it, both an inward and outward force of energy are necessary for all things to exist. Without some sort of inward movement of energy, everything would fly apart. If your chair did not have some inward or "Yin" force holding the molecules together, it would crumble into dust. If the air you breathe had no "Yin" force compressing it together, you would soon find yourself in a vacuum unable to breathe. Without Yin force acting on our air, all the oxygen would be gone and flying outward into infinity.

Similarly, without an outward or "Yang" movement of energy, everything would collapse in upon itself. If your chair had only an inward force, the particles of wood would condense and keep condensing so tightly and so quickly, that it would soon become a particle so dense and heavy and tiny that it would disappear and ultimately sink deep into the Earth.

With these examples, you can see what those Tao masters were trying to teach us: Everything must have both an inward and outward force in order to exist. It must have "inward" to hold it together, and "outward" to have presence and sustain itself.

In the way God works, God's original energy creates and dissolves all things through the interaction of these two energies – inward and outward. From the subatomic level, to the molecular level, to microscopic life, to our bodies, even unto the ends of the universe, everything exists because of the complicated play between these two forces of inward and outward.

Let's look at one of the biggest and most powerful objects in our lives—the sun. The sun is a perfect example of how both inward power and outward power can balance and work together. Where would we be without the immense inward force of our sun's gravity to hold our solar system together? Gravity is the sun's "Yin" force. At the same time, where would be without the outward radiance of the sun to give us heat and light? The heat and light radiating from the sun is its "Yang" force.

If the sun's inward force was even a fraction greater than it is now, our planet couldn't exist. Gravity would suck our Earth into the sun's surface, or at least pull our planet much too close for it to sustain life. If the sun's outward force were any greater, the heat and radiation would destroy life on our planet, and the Sun would burn itself out very quickly, or explode altogether.

As it stands, the sun's gravity pulls in just enough to balance the energy it sends out, keeping it somewhat stable and likely to keep burning for a very long time. The sun provides an example of a balance between inward and outward, Yin and Yang, gravity and radiance. That balance and harmony between these two forces makes the sun the reliable center of our solar system.

Likewise, we have the force of Yin and Yang in our own bodies: we inhale and exhale, drink and perspire, eat and eliminate, in a constant flow of inward and outward that sustains our very life. If one force takes over, our health quickly deteriorates. Imagine if you could drink and drink and drink, but could never urinate or perspire. How long would you live? Or if you could exhale but never inhale.

All life forms we know of, from the cellular level on up, rely on the power of inward and outward to survive and keep themselves in balance. God, the original energy of the universe, is the source of that inward and outward force. Everywhere, in all the many forms it takes, this one universal energy moving inward and outward comprises the backbone and balance of our universe, giving everything structure, meaning, existence and life.

These forces of inward and outward are the two substances that make up the magical flour and water of God's bake shop.

The Whole Universe is Alive
This continual flow of inward and outward everywhere in the universe offers another big clue to the nature of God's original energy: It is always in constant motion.

If you truly think about it, nothing in this universe is ever "still." Everything is in motion. Sub-atomic particles are always moving. The universe itself is expanding and rotating. Even if we sit motionless, our blood is flowing and our cells are busy pulling in nutrients and expelling wastes. Even on the calmest of days, our Earth is both spinning on its axis and orbiting the sun at a speed of several thousand miles per hour.

Why is everything in our universe always moving? Because everything in our universe is made from God's energy, and God's energy is always moving and changing. Why is God's energy always moving and changing? Because it is alive! You see, this is not a dead universe of particles and energy just whirling around mechanically. It is alive!

The reason we think the universe is dead is our faulty perspective. We study theorems on how electrons whirl around protons. We look around and see giant rocks and debris hurtling through empty space. We see bits of light called stars twinkling in a field of darkness. It is all wondrous and beautiful, but in our limited human mind, we consider it merely a display of dead matter obeying laws of physics. Certainly we never consider it to be alive.

How can moons, galaxies and gamma rays, quarks, sand, water and rocky bluffs all be alive? And how can they all be part of one living being, one universal energy? All God?

Let us look at the human body to help us understand: In our body we have many different types of functions and tissues. For example, our bone tissue is so sturdy and hard, we take it for granted as our structural support every day. But since bone tissue grows, moves and changes so slowly, we forget about it and treat it as if it were dead. But our bone tissue is very much alive.

On the other hand, we can hear and feel our heart pounding in our chest. Because we can feel it moving so reliably and so quickly, of course we consider our heart as "alive." But our heart is no more or less alive than our bone tissue. It just moves at a different speed.

Our mind is moving even more quickly still. But we don't think of our thoughts as being alive, because they have no substance that we can see or touch. We treat our thoughts as empty, "dead," or nothingness, just like we consider the endless emptiness of outer space "dead." But even the invisible consciousness that fuels our mind and our thoughts is alive.

What we should see is that bone, heart and thought are all alive and part of ourselves. Your bone is no less a part of you than your heart, and your heart no less a part of you than your memories and thoughts. Even though they all look different, act differently and perform different functions, they are each a facet of who you are. They are all part of what makes you alive.

In the same way, everything in the universe is a living part of this one universal energy. The wide variety of phenomena we see in our universe is only this same one living energy moving in different speeds, different patterns, different phases and combinations of inward and outward. It is all part of the living energy of God. If some parts seem more alive to us than others, it's only because they match up with our bias on what is living and what is not, or our bias on what's real and what's not.

A rock or an asteroid might not seem alive to us. We think they are dead, but they are actually made of that same universal energy moving very slowly. These objects function and "live" at a different frequency than we do. Their energy is not moving quickly enough to give them thoughts or consciousness, or allow them to move independently like we do. But we shouldn't believe our limited perception and regard these slow frequencies of physical matter as dead.

On the opposite end of the spectrum is the fast speeding energy of this living universe. It is invisible to us, so we also wrongly label it as empty or "dead." We call it space, emptiness or nothingness. But space is filled with a finer, subtler, faster form of the same one universal energy. Simply because space looks like "nothing" to us, we underestimate and disregard it. But let's look closer into emptiness so we can learn more about the way God works.

Emptiness is not Empty

So-called "emptiness" does not exist. If there were truly such a thing as emptiness, something would come along to fill it up. What we call nothingness or empty space is not empty. It is filled with higher frequencies of that one universal energy.

Modern science clearly shows us that there are vast ranges of sounds that we cannot hear because they are either above or below the range of our human hearing. Likewise there are countless energies we cannot see because they are outside the narrow spectrum of light our eyes can perceive.

Not only do these higher frequencies of light and sound travel so fast and so fine that we cannot see or hear them, they can become so fast and so fine that they can pass right through solid materials. Think of X-Rays, or gamma rays, or radioactive energy as examples of energies so fast and fine that they can travel through matter.

At the absolute very highest frequencies, where energy travels the fastest, it is so fast and fine that although it appears as nothingness, it can penetrate all things. It is so infinitely fast and fine that it finds its way between the imperceptible gaps within physical matter – the spaces between particles.

This attribute of the most fine, subtle and fast energy of God's universe, is what Lao Tzu meant in the *Tao Te Ching* when he said: "The very subtle can penetrate through all things."

> *"The most refined travels freely,*
> *even through the most dense.*
> *The invisible can penetrate even through*
> *objects with no space."*
> Lao Tzu, *Tao Te Ching*, Chapter 43

We can see many examples of invisible and penetrating energy in today's modern life. Just go to a large airport. You might find a machine that beams invisible energy right through your clothes, and delivers a picture of your naked body to a man behind a desk with a small computer monitor. Lao Tzu could probably never have imagined that!

But we do not have to list all of the many examples of technology that use invisible energy to do their job. You have an example that you carry around all the time: your mind. Mind is one form of this very fast and subtle energy of God. But because we cannot see mind activity, we consider it to be powerless and limited and made of "nothing." Yet like the penetrating power of other forms of fine and subtle energies that travel so incredibly fast, the power of mind can also be very powerful and penetrating.

How fast is it? Just think of a warm sunny day at the beach, and you are there! Then think about the dark side of the moon, or the days of Abraham Lincoln, and you are there — at least in the dimension of your mind.

This ultimate fast and fine energy that can penetrate all things is also what the ancient Tao master Lao Tzu is referring to in the *Tao Te Ching* when he talks about the "weak force" that can overcome the strong.

> "The weak power always overcomes the strong power."
> Lao Tzu, *Tao Te Ching*, Chapter 78

It is not that this force is physically weak in a conventional sense, but that it is energy traveling so fast and at such a high frequency that we cannot feel or see it. In this way only is it weak. In essence, however, this imperceptible energy of nothingness is very powerful – the most powerful force in this living universe.

Lao Tzu's Power of Weak and Small

This invisible yet powerful energy is what the old masters mean when they claim the "small" can overcome the large. "Weak" and "small" were adjectives they used, but it's important to understand their true meaning. Again, the masters didn't mean physically weak or small: they were trying to convey a concept.

There is an old legend about a scholar who traveled many hundreds of miles to meet with a well-known temple master in order to debate the spiritual teachings of his day. When the scholar finally arrived at the master's temple chambers, he challenged the old monk, saying: "Many of your spiritual teachings make no sense and are completely illogical."

The master calmly replied, "Indeed? Which teachings do you judge as wrong?"

The scholar replied, "For one example, your scrolls say that the very small can fit inside the very large and the very large can fit inside the very small. That is impossible! Anybody can see that I can place something small inside something large. But how can I place something that is very large inside something that is very small? It simply cannot be done. I dare you to show me how you can fit something very large into something very small."

The master nodded and thoughtfully replied. "Scholar, you are right. That teaching is ridiculous and illogical. I don't know if I would be able to show you that or not. After all you must know exactly what you are talking about because you have read over a thousand books, isn't that true?"

"Yes, I have. I have read well over a thousand books," replied the scholar. "That is why I challenge this ridiculous teaching."

The master nodded. "And I imagine that all those thousands of books that you have read to make you so smart must have filled an entire room, maybe even a very large library! I wonder where they all are now and how you got all those large books into such a small space," said the master, reaching over and touching the center of the scholar's forehead.

The arrogant scholar suddenly realized the master's superior wisdom and felt very ashamed, bowing low in humility.

So that you become much wiser than that foolish scholar, let's talk more about weak and small. When Lao Tzu describes the power of Tao as "very weak" or "very small," he means a power so small that we cannot see it, and so weak that we cannot feel it in a physical sense. It is that power of the universal energy traveling so fast and at such a high frequency that we can only describe it as "nothingness" because our own mind and our own senses are so limited. This is the real power of nothingness or the "power of the void" that Lao Tzu is trying to convey in so many chapters of the *Tao Te Ching*.

Even though it is all-powerful and everywhere, the substance of God's ultimate energy is so "small" and so "weak," we don't even realize it's there. That's why Lao Tzu says:

> *"Heaven's net is ever large and wide.*
> *Though its meshes are coarse,*
> *yet nothing slips through."*
>   Lao Tzu, *Tao Te Ching*, Chapter 73

He is saying that although Tao's net stretches everywhere, we can't see it. Just as if you were caught in a net whose holes were so vast you couldn't see them, you wouldn't really know you were inside that net.

In Lao Tzu's day, they did not have the same scientific knowledge and vocabulary that we do. Today we can point to X-rays, radio waves and airport scanners as examples of invisible power. However, when Lao Tzu tries to describe the invisible power of Tao, he uses words and examples from his world, like a "net with wide meshes," or "weak power" or "Tao is like water."

Yet we shouldn't think that our scientific understanding and technological examples make us wiser than Lao Tzu. In fact, our reliance on the language and ideas of science often hinders us. Why? You see, trying to match these highest truths about the way God works to our human understanding of physics can also pose a trap. It can limit us.

The One Universal Energy is Intelligent

When we use the ideas of energy and physics to help us understand how the ultimate power of the universe works, there is usually one big characteristic of Tao that we've overlooked. This one factor transcends physics as we know it. This factor is intelligence.

The one energy that comprises everything everywhere is an intelligent and living being. That is why science always reaches a limit in its ability to explain and understand the universe around us. It never factors in the super-intelligence of God.

The origin of the universe is a "super ultimate intelligence." That intelligence permeates everything in this entire network of the universe to a greater or lesser degree.

One reason understanding the super-intelligence of God is so hard for us is because this same intelligence is precisely what we ourselves are made of. We are made of this same substance, this same intelligent, one universal living energy. Our very mind that enables us to participate in science is fueled by the same innate substance comprising the whole universe. Our consciousness and intelligence is a small isolated piece, a downgraded copy of that one universal conscious and intelligent energy.

We don't understand that our connection to that Source is the root of our intelligence. When we cannot even see or understand where our own intelligence comes from, then we limit our understanding of the universe. That's why we cannot see that everything around us is also created from the same living and intelligent energy.

This, in the end, is why we have found few answers to those big questions: because our universe cannot be understood by the so-called "scientific method" alone. We humans hammer away at all the big questions of birth, death, existence, time and space, armed with our relatively small concepts of physics and our artificially isolated and finite minds.

All of our little rules governing science and logic have evolved from centuries of limited human understanding. These rules are embedded deep within our human thinking, and make us unable to understand the higher truths about the way God works. We have to step outside of our limited mind and all its limited rules in order to get a better look at the truth about God.

After all, the little amount of the truth we think we know is defined by the limitations of Earth. For example, we think we know how water behaves. It can turn into steam, liquid or ice. But if you travel outside of the Earth's atmosphere, water can behave quite differently. In outer space, there are several exponentially colder versions of water that are called "Ice3" "Ice4" or "Ice10." These other dimensions of ice behave quite differently than the ice floating around in your glass of water.

When you spill your glass of water here on Earth, you can predict it will run all over the floor. But when you spill your glass of water out in space, something altogether different happens. Just as we must let go of our earthbound rules to understand how water behaves in space, we have to let go of our earthbound logic and rules to understand the ways of God.

Let's say we have a very powerful telescope that can see far into the universe. In order for it to work at its best, we still have to move that telescope up into space, above the clouds, moisture, light pollution and distortion, so that what we can see is clear.

That's why you'll find so many astronomical observatories perched on mountaintops, or telescopes built into satellites. They try to rise above the distortion of Earth's atmosphere.

Our mind is like that powerful telescope. It is a sophisticated and hard-working instrument, but we have to lift it above the distortion of our limited world's rules and logic in order to understand the super-intelligence of God.

This God, this nothingness, is beyond our comprehension. It is not subject to our physics or logic. Our rules don't apply. Next to this Origin, we are pitifully naïve. We try to make sense of God by comparing God to things we know, because comparing it to things we already know makes us feel comfortable. But we really can't compare anything to God, we can only come up with partial analogies.

That's why Lao Tzu described this Tao as "*Bu Xiao.*" Bu Xiao means "nothing like it." It means you cannot compare it to anything we know. When it comes to understanding God, it's as if we are floating in space. We are in total darkness with no reference point. In space, we start to wonder which way is up, because we are used to up and down in reference to our earthbound idea of the truth. But in space, up and down don't really exist anymore in the way we understand them.

Similarly, we try to compare our earthbound ideas to "*Bu Xiao,*" but they won't work. No matter how we talk and try, we cannot make sense of it. It is virtually impossible for us to understand how intelligent and indestructible God is. It's so elusive and vague to us.

So how can we understand the Origin and its intelligence? By getting rid of our own artificial, human, earthbound intelligence and reconnecting with that piece of God's intelligence inside of us. Only then can we see and know the truth. That's what Lao Tzu managed to do and what he tried to tell us about.

Lao Tzu Describes What God is Like

Chapter 21 of the *Tao Te Ching* is a very important chapter, because it is the first time in the *Tao Te Ching* where Lao Tzu tries to describe the Tao and what it's really like. He's giving us a first hand account from his own meditation on what he experienced when he successfully connected back to that original God.

> *"The Great Te follows nothing but Tao,*
> *though Tao is elusive and subtle.*
> *It seems elusive and subtle,*
> *and yet within it is an image.*
> *It seems subtle and elusive,*
> *and yet within it is a form.*
> *It appears vague and subtle,*
> *and yet within it is an essence.*
> *This essence is very real,*
> *and therein lays a message.*
> *From the very beginning until now,*
> *its name has never been erased.*

*Thus I can see and perceive everything within creation.
How do I know everything within creation?
Because of this."*
                    Lao Tzu, Tao Te Ching, Chapter 21

This chapter seems very hard to understand and very mysterious. Of course it is! Remember, trying to understand and describe God is no easy task. We have to step outside of our usual way of understanding.

Lao Tzu first refers to something called the "Great Te." That "Great Te" is part of what connects us to God. You see, inside of us, we have something that the old Tao masters called "Te." Te (pronounced *"day"*) is that piece of God inside of you and me that connects each of us to that big network of God's energy. We all have a piece of God inside of us, because we are each made of that one universal energy. (Even the Bible talks about this when it says we are made in the image and likeness of God, or when Jesus says, "The kingdom of God is inside you.") With Te, we have a small copy of that Tao right inside of us.

And Lao Tzu says the "Great Te follows nothing but Tao." That means the Te inside us must follow Tao because it's a piece of Tao. So if we can find our Te, we instantly have the key to following Tao, since Te must follow Tao.

Lao Tzu understood that he could use his "Te" as a means to reach back to connect with God through meditation. He left this chapter as a record to tell us that he made it! He wanted to describe this journey so that others would know what to expect when they tried to contact God. He left Chapter 21 as a little road map for our journey. With Chapter 21 in hand, you will have Lao Tzu's experience to measure against when you start to meditate on your own journey back to God. "First it's subtle, then vague, then an essence, then a message...."

It's as if I described my trip to Chicago in a letter to you so that when you drove there from California, you'd understand when you were getting closer. "From Missouri, keep going north on I-55 and when you get closer you will see factories. Then there will be suburbs, and then in the distance you will see very tall buildings reaching for the sky. Keep going and beyond those buildings you will see a vast lake that stretches as far as the eye can see. When you can see the lake, you're there!" When you take my letter with you and drive towards Chicago, you will understand "Oh! There's a bunch of factories. I must be getting closer. Look! I see the tops of skyscrapers in the distance. Oh! Just past those buildings is a big stretch of water. This must be Chicago, just like Master Liao's letter says."

On his way back to God through meditation, Lao Tzu experienced something "vague," "subtle" and "elusive." When you go back to Tao, it's hard to understand at first, even for Lao Tzu! In fact, one way to know you are really heading in the right direction toward God is that as you get closer, it will seem subtle and elusive. Remember, God is far beyond what our human mind can conceive and understand. So to us, the Tao, the way of God, is so elusive and so weak. Remember, weak means very refined, very tiny, almost as if it's not existent, so we cannot feel it. It's vague!

Lao Tzu kept poking that vagueness and subtleness and found an essence. That means he landed on something real. It had substance. When he found that essence, he kept going and inside there was a "message." When something has a message, it means that the source of that message has thought, ideas and can communicate. What Lao Tzu is trying to say is "Hey! It's intelligent!" This essence, this backbone energy of the universe is intelligent.

Then later Lao Tzu says that it is "because of this, I can see and perceive everything within creation." The only reason we human beings are intelligent is because we have a piece of that same God inside of us! Our intelligence is accomplished through that Te. Without Te, that essence of God's intelligence, you would be unable to think, perceive or be aware. You would be like a rock or a vegetable. You owe your intelligence to the fact that God has intelligence.

If you are going to make a wrist watch that can tell time, you need various watch parts. You especially need a part that can meter the passing seconds, minutes, and hours. You need a "time part" in order for a watch to give you the time. Likewise, if you are going to create an intelligent human being, you need a "smart part" to give it intelligence. That "smart part" is a piece of God.

Warning to those who smugly think, "There is no God. Where is God? Nobody can prove to me that there is a God." The only way people can even ask such questions is by using their very own little tarnished piece of God inside of them. If you had no piece of God inside you, such questions would never arise. Your mind would be unable to stretch far enough to even imagine such a fathomless idea like God!

Unless you have the intelligence and life energy of God inside of you, nothing exists to you. Our senses – hearing, smelling, seeing, feeling, tasting – don't happen in our ears, nose, eyes or mouth. They actually happen in our brain. You sniff and molecules trigger certain nerves that travel to the brain, and you say "Ah, I smell roses!" Or you open your eyes and look out the window and see that it's cloudy today. That's because your eyes sent a picture to your brain and your brain assembled and interpreted that picture to let you know "it's cloudy."

This is still only part of the story. A cadaver in a lab has eyes, ears, and a nose, each of which are hooked up by nerve cells to a brain. But that cadaver can't see, hear or smell a thing! The only way your brain can receive and interpret the signals from your nose and eyes is through the living and intelligent consciousness of life energy. That conscious intelligent life energy is ultimately made possible by Te. Te is responsible for all of our five senses as well as our ability to think.

Today's scientists can't really answer the question, "What makes human beings conscious?" or "What makes human beings aware and intelligent?" Those, too, are questions our limited human science can never answer. They can map the brain, measure neurotransmitters, study psychology and personality theory, and talk all they want, but no scientist will be able to tell you exactly what makes us conscious and alive or where in our body the origin of consciousness and life resides. That is because what makes us conscious and alive is that piece of the one living universal power of God inside of us – our Te.

God's Power to Materialize
The Book of Genesis in the Bible tells us how God creates: "Let there be Light!" "Let there be Water!" "Let there be Life!" The ability of God to create is instantaneous. When God thinks, it *is*. When Tao thinks heat, it's hot. When Tao thinks cold, it's cold. If destruction is deemed necessary, watch out!

Imagine if everything you dream came true. Because God's thinking instantly materializes, it's as if our universe is the "Grand Dream" of God. The universe is constantly unfolding like a big full-scale dream.

God's dream is so powerful that if God dreams it wants an object as hot as one million degrees Celsius, it instantly *is*. If God wants light – there's light. If God wants water– there's water. It just creates, effortlessly. That's how powerful the Origin is.

That's what it's like in the realm of God. When this highest intelligence thinks or dreams, its energy knows instantly and exactly what to do to materialize it. It can even blow up and create an entire universe in one "Big Bang."

God's energy is a subtle, invisible and intelligent force that fills everything everywhere in our universe. That invisible force can instantly manifest the will and dream of God. *That's* the weak and small force that we call emptiness. Now do you see why Lao Tzu told us that this weak and empty force is so powerful? This is why you have to treat nothingness as the most ever-powerful something.

This is hard for us to really conceive, because our thinking is a low level lousy copy of God's way of thinking. We have a piece of that intelligent energy of God inside, but it is buried under layers of heavy insulation and is so slow. Our thinking takes place at such a lower level, we don't have that power. Our concepts are hollow. When we think "let there be light," it's just wishful thinking.

At our low level, we have to go through the material world in order to "create" something. We cannot say "Let there be a chair." No. If you have an idea that you want a chair, you have to go through so much work! You have to saw down trees, work the lumber, hammer and saw and sand and varnish, just to create something as simple as a chair. This is because we lost that connection to the infinite mind of God. We lost that ability to instantly materialize what we need.

Our mental powers are ridiculously stupid compared to God. God uses "non-action" to accomplish anything and everything, anywhere and anytime it wants. God doesn't need action and labor like we do. God just has an idea and that is enough. But because we are at such a low-level and are squeezed out of that original dimension, we cannot do this. We cannot use God's non-action power. We have to resort to action. We are in this dumb dimension of physical matter. We can think an idea, but we have to make it real by creating from materials we can find around us.

Guess who also created that material? God. It's like we are kids whose mother put them in a sandbox, and filled it up with sand so we can make things. Instead of being like magical pastry chefs, we are like toddlers in the kitchen, spilling flour and water all over the place and making a pasty gluey mess while we try to play "baker."

God is One Piece

God's energy creates and sustains everything everywhere at all times. Even if we don't realize it or believe it, we are right "in it." Since the entire universe and everything in it is inside that network of God, God is one piece. This is the "uncarved block" Lao Tzu talks about in some translations of the *Tao Te Ching*. Since God is one piece, that is why nothing can escape this vast network of Tao – nothing can be carved off of the block.

Science simply isn't able to comprehend everything in the universe as one piece. It focuses on the very small material portion of our universe.

When God makes material, he condenses that nothingness together so that it's dense. That condensed energy forms our material universe. But the part of our universe that makes up the "material world" is a very small part of the whole piece.

God is like this entire piece of paper on the page that you are reading. If you folded over or "dog-eared" the top corner of this book page and glued it down, that little denser triangle would represent the material part of our universe. The remaining flat page would be the rest of God that we cannot see. Science is preoccupied with that little dog-eared corner, thinking that is all there is, and ignoring the rest of the page.

If they could see God as the backbone of everything in the universe, and the universe as one piece, they might look at gravity in a different way. After all if I'm one piece, and I pull part of myself together into a particle or I pull in to make a planet, it creates a force pulling on the rest of the net surrounding it. That *"pull"* forces something else to move in to fill that space. Right now, reach over and pinch together an inch or so of skin on the top of your hand. You'll notice that the rest of the skin around where you're pinching is automatically pulled toward that spot. That's because your skin is one piece.

This understanding would also change how we understand time. The closer we get to the center of God, the more time feels like it is slowing down; while the further from the center we are, the faster time flies by. Time, like God, is one piece. But it can be condensed together or stretched out.

Those old Taoists wrote down many mysteries without explaining the truth behind them plainly and clearly. It is because God is one piece that those old masters can say: "The very far and distant are close by," or "past and future are the same." It is because God is one piece that Lao Tzu can say, "Something and nothingness are like two equal things." My desk is strong material, but it comes from the formless. The atoms that make up my desk are like nothing individually. "Strong" simply means taking a lot of weakness and compressing it together.

This Original energy is indestructible, forever and immortal. We are in the material world and slower than that original and highest energy frequency of nothingness, that's why we are not immortal. Our material dimension is very slow and far away from the highest frequency of God.

Although you are in a material body, you can never escape this invisible network of Tao. You can only lose your awareness of it. We must use that emptiness in order to restore that awareness, to return back to Tao — for the dimension of God is forever and holds all the answers we seek.

But there are many other layers of existence, other beings and other energy between our material world and the one true God, just as there are many different frequencies of energy between physical matter and nothingness. To understand the relationship between ourselves and God, we must also understand the spiritual dimension.

PART TWO:
The Spiritual Dimension

道

The Spiritual Dimension

All of the major religions contain footprints of similar truths. They are all using different words and different stories to try to tell us some of the same things. One common footprint in Christianity, Buddhism, Taoism, Islam and even ancient Egyptian religions is the idea that there are other places beyond this Earthly dimension.

Many of those old religions talk about some type of heaven or hell or spiritual worlds outside of our everyday world. In those old teachings, these worlds are populated by angels, immortals, demons, ghosts, or other types of supernatural beings. Sometimes these other worlds even have homes, palaces, kings, queens, and bureaucracies, much like we have on earth. And sometimes tales tell that these other spiritual beings come down to our dimension where they can either help us or cause trouble.

This idea of other worlds or other "heavenly" dimensions is so common, it is important not to reject this idea, but to meditate and penetrate further into what those old religious teachings and folk legends were trying to tell us.

It is very hard for us to conceive of another spiritual dimension. To give an example of how hard it is, let's say several fish are swimming around in the only world they know – their little pond. To them, the universe ends where the water ends. They believe that beyond the water there is nothing, because they believe nothing can exist without water. Anything outside of the water doesn't make sense to them.

One day, the fish are happily swimming in their pond when Sam the fish sees a delicious looking worm dangling in the water and bites it. All of a sudden, while the other fish watch, Sam just disappears right out of the universe! *Whoosh!* Very mysterious!

Meanwhile, our fish Sam is experiencing something very strange. He is pulled up by a mysterious force outside of the water. He sees an odd creature with very big eyes looking down at him. He feels a strange dry sensation that he cannot even describe, because he's never felt "dry" before. There is very bright light all around him. He's scared and confused and feels a terrible pain in his mouth, and then the pain is gone and suddenly he is back in the water again.

In that dimension outside of the water, a fisherman caught a fish in a pond. He grabs the fish at the end of his line and takes the hook out of its mouth. He looks the fish over carefully, but finally says, "Eh! Too small!" and throws the fish back into the water.

Splash! Suddenly, all of the other fish see Sam magically reappear out of nowhere and are amazed! They swim over to ask Sam what happened. Sam the fish just had a "near-death" experience! He went to another dimension!

But when Sam the fish tries to explain, he sounds foolish: "First I saw a white light, and then big eyes, *glub, blub*, God looked at me *glub, glub,* terrible pain and squeezing, *bubble, bubble,* no water, *glub, gurgle,* terrible loud noises, pain in my mouth, and then splash, I came back..." Sam has a hard time describing his experience, because there are no fish words, no fish ideas that can match what he felt and saw.

Sam tells his story to everyone. The other fish think he's crazy, and soon the rest of the pond agrees. Nobody listens to Sam's story after awhile, and he spends more and more time alone swimming by himself, thinking about his strange experience, trying to make sense of it all.

Why don't all the other fish believe what Sam tells them? Well partly because Dr. Fish, the smartest fish in the pond who graduated with a PhD in pond physics from Lake Harvard University, told everyone that the universe ends at the water's edge. Therefore Sam must be crazy. There's nothing up there outside of the water!

We're a lot like those fish in the pond. The spiritual dimension exists, whether or not we believe it and whether or not we can perceive it. Like it or not, it's there. But it can be very hard for us to describe and understand it.

First of all, understand that the spiritual dimension is not in some far off place beyond the clouds or under the earth. It is right here. We are right inside of it. Our dimension and the spiritual dimension overlap. Right now, our awareness is tuned in like a radio dial to the frequency of earth and human life. We call this reality. But if we turn our radio dial just a little to one side, we change stations completely and receive a whole new program. Likewise, if we turn our dial just a little bit one way, we are in heaven. If we turn just a little bit the other way, we are in hell.

Like our radio analogy, many stations are broadcasting at the same time over the airwaves. Whether we tune into one or the other doesn't mean the other stations are no longer there. Those other radio programs are still broadcasting loud and strong right next to our bandwidth; we're just not currently tuned into them. This is how it is with the spiritual dimension and its many layers.

In our material dimension, we experience everything as opaque and substantial. That other dimension is a "transparent" dimension. Everything is transparent. In this dimension if I'm thinking nasty thoughts, it's hidden. Nobody knows unless I speak or do something. But up there in the transparency dimension, everybody knows immediately. All thoughts register in that dimension and everybody knows what everyone is thinking because they are all connected.

This transparency dimension is where you are before birth and after death. You spend much more time in that dimension than in this one. That's why kids are constantly asking "Mommy, do you love me?" because they don't know. Kids are used to that transparency dimension and this dimension we live in feels very strange to them.

Here on Earth, I can only see time in a linear sequence. I have to watch the movie of my life and the world around me unfold from beginning to end, frame by frame, as the movie projector spins the reel around. In that other dimension, it's different. It's as if I can see the whole film in an instant. In that dimension there is no past or future, no here or there. Our version of time and space is almost ridiculous compared to how it looks in that dimension.

Since it overlaps with ours, this transparent spiritual dimension can have a profound affect on our life energy. That's why it's important to understand as best we can how it works. We need to understand so we can find the right signal we are looking for, the right dimension to tune into. Which channel do we need in order to find the ultimate God? Is your radio dial turned to the station broadcasting hell or heaven? Can you find God's signal, or is your dial stuck?

All Beings Move Out From and Return to the Center

God's original energy is like the Center of this vast creation. The Center of this energy vibrates at such a fast and fine frequency, it is completely pure. That Center is the one true God.

God extends its energy outward to form everything in the universe. As the substance of God extends out from itself, the further from the center it goes, the more it starts to slow down. It slows down until it reaches the end of its extension, then it turns around to come back. Because God is one piece, if part of God moves away it doesn't separate, it stretches away like a rubber band. Whatever stretches out from that center will only go so far before it slows down and starts pulling back in again.

Everything that goes out from that Center of God will one day return and come back toward the Center.

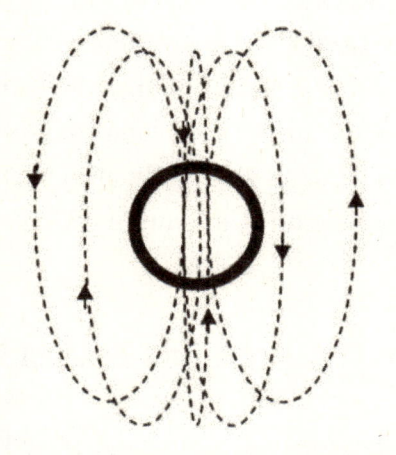

**Everything goes out from
and returns to the Center**

God's energy is always moving, always circulating, in and out from that Center. This circulation, in and out, from fast to the boundary of slow where it stops and turns around to come back again, is how God's energy forms and fills the many layers, densities and dimensions of the spiritual and physical world.

In Chapter 16 of the *Tao Te Ching*, Lao Tzu says that after you are so still, calm and pure, you can touch that original network where you will see the 10,000 things in circular sequence.

> *"Attain to the utmost inward weakness.*
> *Focus firmly in the purest state of stillness*
> *Suddenly, the ten thousand things will appear*
> *in circular sequence.*
> *And then everything will develop and flourish*
> *and then return to the source of the void."*
> Lao Tzu, *Tao Te Ching*, Chapter 16

What did he mean by that? Lao Tzu is describing what he saw when he entered that spiritual and transparent dimension. While in that dimension, he could see and know everything at once. What he saw was everything in creation revolving in a circle. Everything in every dimension has the same root, the same origin. That's why the 10,000 things move in circular sequence — they are revolving around one Center. Every created thing not only comes out from God, but also goes back and returns to God.

> *"Something mysteriously formed,*
> *even before heaven and earth;*
> *In the loneliness and the void,*
> *standing alone and unchanging;*
> *Ever present and moving ceaselessly;*
> *It is the mother of heaven and earth.*

> *I do not know its name. Let's just call it Tao.*
> *For lack of a better word, let's call it the Great.*
> *So great, let's call it the disappearing.*
> *Disappearing into far away,*
> *let's call it the far away.*
> *Having gone so far, eventually it returns,*
> *So let's also call it the return."*
>   Lao Tzu, *Tao Te Ching*, Chapter 25

Since everything comes from God and returns to God, you and every other being in the universe are always in one of three conditions with respect to God: you are either moving towards God, moving away from God or staying at the same distance.

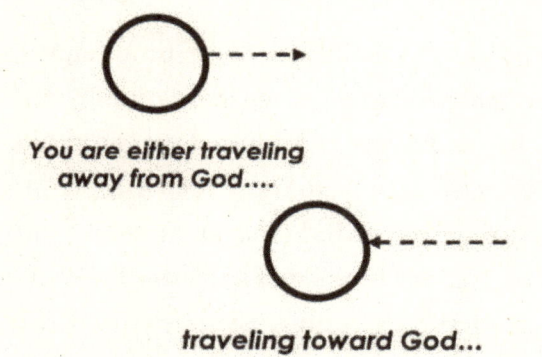

You are either traveling away from God....

traveling toward God...

...or staying at the same distance away from God.

This ongoing dynamic process is happening to everything in creation. Everything in creation is raising or slowing down its energy frequency — moving closer to God or moving farther away or spinning around and around the Center. That's why this universe is dynamic, unpredictable and always changing. It is a churning, revolving "soup" that's continuously moving around the Center of God.

The closer you move in the direction toward God, the more you experience a higher vibration of life, power, consciousness, intelligence and truth. The further away you are, the slower and weaker your vibration of life, consciousness, intelligence and truth becomes. Moving closer to God feels like "heaven," while moving further from God can feel like suffering or "hell."

If that's the case, then why would anything want to be moving away from God? Why do some things drop from a high level to a low level? Does God banish or punish earthly or spiritual beings, kick them down or send them away? No. It's the *rule* that does this, not God.

The rule is this: If your energy is heavy and slow, it sinks down to lower levels and further away from the Center. If your energy is pure and light, you float up to higher levels and move closer to the Center. It is the rule of energy "frequency" that defines whether you are moving closer to God, moving away from God or staying at the same distance. It isn't a result of God being cruel or punishing, even though it may look like that from a limited human perspective.

We make many choices in our daily life that are either moving our energy closer to God or moving us away. Today you might help someone else from a pure heart, and as a result your energy becomes purer and moves closer to God. Tomorrow you can get angry or burn up a lot of energy complaining, and you'll end up moving away again.

It's not God who decides this for you, it's a result of that rule. Therefore what you choose, do, think, say and practice can have a determining effect in the direction you go with respect to God, and how far you go in that direction.

Different Layers and Levels of Energy

God is the universal energy that creates and extends through the whole universe and through its wide variety of inhabitants. The best analogy we can use to describe why there is such a wide variety of life forms and material objects in our universe is that they are all vibrating at different frequencies.

If we look at our world, we can illustrate it this way: A rock is vibrating at a much slower frequency than a tree. A tree vibrates at a slower frequency than a horse. And a horse is vibrating at a slower frequency than a human. And humans are vibrating slower than the spiritual dimension, and much slower than God.

Whether or not an object has "life," whether it has "consciousness," or whether it has "intelligence," depends on whether it has enough energy and is vibrating fast enough to give it life, consciousness or intelligence.

For example, a rock is made from that same one intelligent substance of God, but it is vibrating at such a slow frequency that it doesn't have anywhere near enough energy to give it what we would call "life," consciousness or intelligence. It doesn't feel or think anything. It doesn't have the capacity to even know it exists. But it is still connected to that original network. As part of the solid material world, it sits in the outermost reaches, the slowest end of God's energy spectrum.

Somewhere between the mineral kingdom and the plant kingdom are various amoeba and cell-like creatures. We consider these the simplest and lowest forms of life we know. These simple life forms are vibrating just fast enough that they barely cross over that boundary into the category we call "living beings." But even though they have life energy, or "Chi," they do not vibrate fast enough to have what we call "consciousness" or "mind."

A plant is vibrating fast enough that it definitely has life energy. A plant may also have a simple level of consciousness that we can't quite understand. On some cellular level a plant may sense that it exists and "knows" what to do to adapt itself to certain changes in its environment, but it doesn't really have a "mind."

A horse's energy is vibrating at a high enough level that it most definitely has life energy and consciousness. A horse knows it exists. It is also vibrating fast enough to have an intelligent mind that can think simple thoughts and even have simple emotions or feelings. And yet its mind is not at the higher level of a human being's mind.

(For those that think this description treats animals in an unfair or unflattering way, we should remember that our high-speed and clever mind is like a double-edged sword. Even though animals and plants don't have the clever mind that we do, they also don't have the confusion and mental pollution human beings suffer. That's why, even though they vibrate at a lower frequency than ours, animals can often pick up much more information directly from God's network of energy through their unbiased instincts and feelings. They don't have the burden of a mixed-up mind. We can learn a lot from them.)

Humans are vibrating so fast that we are the highest level of being in this Earth's material dimension. With our high level of consciousness and our very versatile mind, we live right at the boundary of the material and spiritual worlds. We are vibrating so fast, we are right next to it.

Even though we humans like to think we are the most sophisticated creature in the universe, the ladder or layers of different levels of being doesn't suddenly jump from us all the way to the ultimate God. There are many levels, many spiritual beings, many small "gods," filling up many layers and frequencies of the spiritual dimension between the human level and God.

To illustrate this, we know from our study of physics that there are many frequencies and types of invisible energy. These many forms of energy range from slow to fast. Sound is much slower than light and light itself is broken up into a wide spectrum of colors. Electricity is yet another form of energy.

Here on Earth, we can see a similar analogy in the many stages of life between an amoeba and a human being. There are literally tens of thousands of different species of life on our planet.

Likewise, there are also many levels of spiritual energy and spiritual worlds between human beings and God. These other beings vibrate even faster than we do and are invisible to us.

In higher spiritual dimensions there are beings we refer to as "evil," as well as beings we refer to as "angels." There are many levels of these higher evil and angelic beings, these lesser "gods," all the way up to the true God. Each spiritual form originates from and is made from the intelligent energy of God, just like we are. They have a piece of that intelligence inside of them, but like us, they are vibrating at a frequency slower than that of the original God.

The inhabitants of these different layers and levels of the spiritual dimension have different levels of God's intelligent power. Their minds can do and perceive things that human beings cannot. The range of their power depends on how far they are from the Center of God's power.

As God's energy radiates out from the center, it starts out very fast and gradually slows down before returning again. Let's work from the Center outward and see how God's power starts to degrade to form the different levels of beings in our universe.

Level one, the Center of God's power, is "think and create." This is the ultimate level of the one true God. God thinks "Let there be a mountain!" and from nothingness, suddenly there is a mountain. This is an example of the highest level of God's power.

Level two of God's power is slightly downgraded. It is "think and annihilate." God's energy at this level thinks "Let there be no more mountain!" Instantaneously, the mountain disappears into nothingness. It is the power of God to erase what is disagreeable in respect to God's ultimate idea and purpose.

Level three of God's power is "think and transform." Instead of annihilating what is disagreeable, this power changes what has already been created to a different form. So God can think, "Let the mountain be smaller" and it's smaller. Or God can think, "Let the mountain be bigger and purple!" and the mountain grows bigger and becomes purple. Or God can think, "Change this tree into a mountain!" and the transformation immediately takes place.

Level four of God's power is "think and move from here to there!" So God can think "Move this mountain from the east over to the west." Instantly, the mountain will be transported from east to west.

The levels of power continue downward. Level five is "think and multiply" whereby this power of God can make duplicate copies of anything. Level six is the power of restoration whereby God's power works to heal or repair damages to what has already been

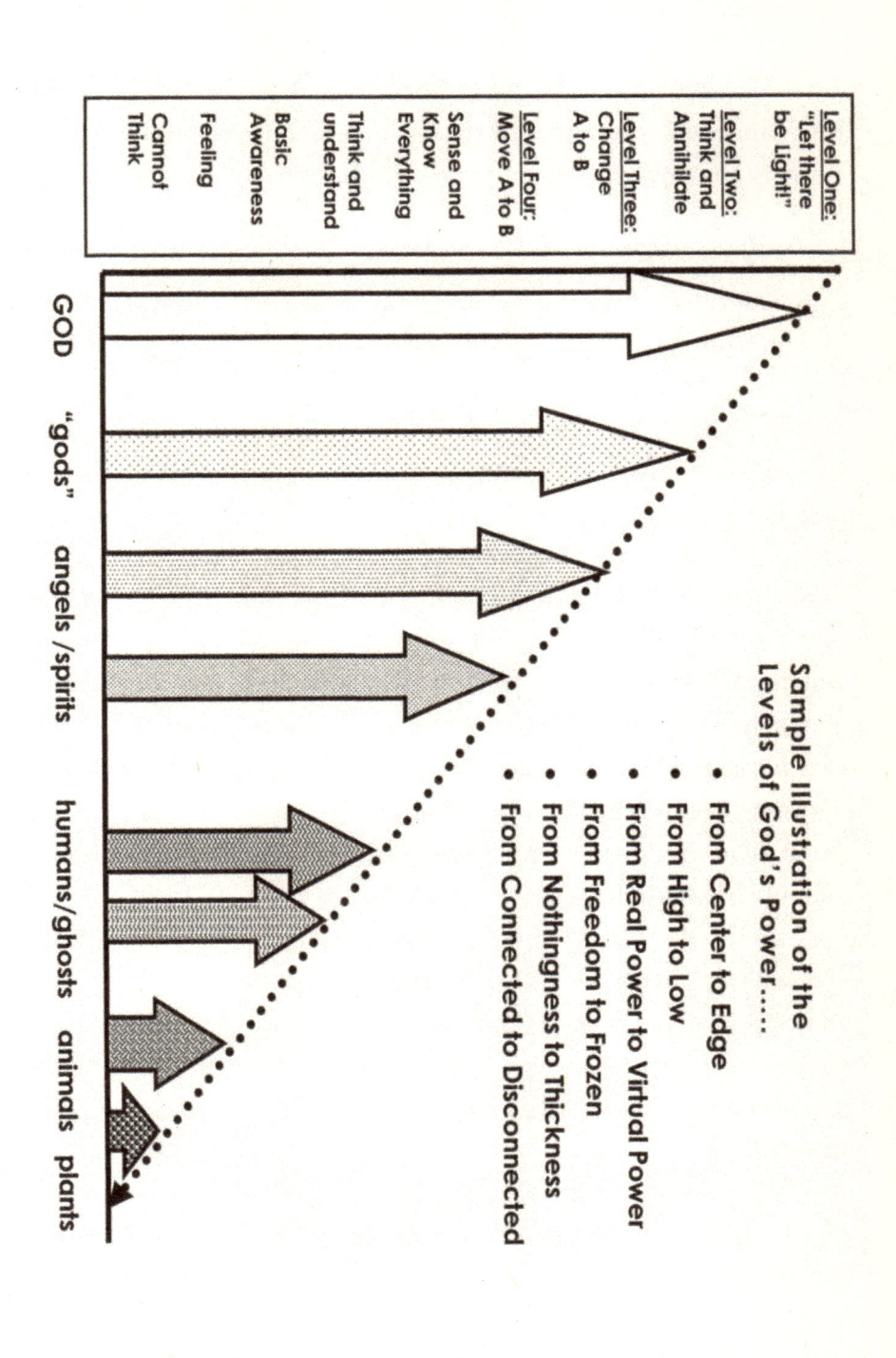

THE SPIRITUAL DIMENSION   59

Level One:
"Let there be Light!"

Level Two:
Think and Annihilate

Level Three:
Change A to B

Level Four:
Move A to B

Sense and Know Everything

Think and understand

Basic Awareness

Feeling

Cannot Think

GOD   "gods"   angels/spirits   humans/ghosts   animals   plants

Sample Illustration of the Levels of God's Power......

- From Center to Edge
- From High to Low
- From Real Power to Virtual Power
- From Freedom to Frozen
- From Nothingness to Thickness
- From Connected to Disconnected

created. Level seven is the power to repel and defend against resistance to God's power or to resist the decline of energy. Level eight is the power to harmonize, seeking the perfect within the imperfect.

The different layers in the spiritual dimension are filled with beings who may boast some of these powers.

Our mind is also made from God's intelligent power, but it is at the very low end of God's power spectrum. If God's power starts at Level 1, then it's as if we are at level "k." We humans are at the very "tail-end" of God's intelligence. Our mind power is so ridiculously low, that we cannot do what God can do.

But in our dimension we hold a very unique place. We human beings are high enough that we live at the boundary of the physical and spiritual world. Because we are at that boundary, we have a unique capability. If we can raise our frequency just a little bit, we can communicate with the spiritual dimension and the dimension of the original God.

We are very different in that respect from plants and animals. In our physical world, plants and animals have life energy, what we call *Chi*, just like we do, but they don't have *Te* (that higher and faster piece of God's energy that gives us our amazing minds.)

On the other hand, beings in those spiritual dimensions have Te, but they don't have Chi – life energy. Without Chi, they cannot live, function, change or create things in the material world. We humans are unique in that we have both! That is why human life is so special. The human dimension is a "layer" or "phase" that energy passes through on its way to or from God. It is a special dimension where we have a chance to repair that energy. With *both* Chi and Te, we have the right tools we need to change and improve ourselves, raise our energy and connect back to God.

Many Spiritual Levels – Many "gods"

There are many beings that function like lower spiritual "gods" underneath the ultimate God. That poses a problem for us. When we are working hard to tune into the signal of the one ultimate God, we can mistake one of these lower spiritual beings for the real God. And if you are on this spiritual journey back to Tao, you will most likely run into a few of these small "gods" on your way there.

Remember that just like you, and everyone and everything else in this universe, spiritual beings are in one of three conditions: Spiritual beings are either moving away from God, moving toward God or staying at the same distance.

Unfortunately, when you connect with one of these spiritual beings or lower fake "gods," it can be very hard to tell which direction they are heading. You might get fooled into thinking that you are contacting the real God, when actually you've just connected to a very powerful spiritual being that happens to be traveling away from God. This can be disastrous.

Let's say we look up in the sky and see a jet plane for the first time. What a miracle! We've never seen anything so fast and so marvelous. We worship that plane in awe. But in the sky there can be passenger planes, cargo planes, war planes on their way to drop bombs, planes from the USA or planes from China. We can't tell from our ground level what kind of plane it is, where it's going, or what its purpose is. We're just so amazed that we worship the very first one we see, or maybe we worship them all.

Evil and angel both need and use God's power to power what they do — just like a passenger jet and a fighter jet both need the same fuel, need the same air for lift, and need to fly in the same sky. But those two planes have a different purpose. They are going in completely different directions. Now when I stand on the ground, I can't know all this when I look up and see a jet. I worship that jet even though I don't know what its purpose is or where it is going. I just love the fact that it can fly around and do such fancy stuff. See how short-sighted I am, stuck here at ground level?

If you become enchanted with the miracles, powers and sensations of the spiritual dimension, you might wrongly worship a fake god that's traveling even farther away from the real Center. That's bad news for you, because by the time you figure out you've been worshipping the wrong god, it may take you a very long time to make your way back and head in the right direction again.

Equally dangerous is that you can end up worshipping a half-way god who's just parked there in that spiritual dimension orbiting around the Center at a consistent distance from God. If you hook up to a halfway god and park there and circulate there with that god, you may forget about your ultimate goal. It can feel and seem so nice. Just like if I get a nice job, nice house, and nice food, why should I move or change anything? Why should I keep pressing on toward the real God?

Yes, there are many spiritual so-called "gods." Those that are truly good will point you toward the real God. They won't want you to get stuck idling there. Misleading you or stopping you would hurt their spiritual progress as well as yours. After all, these "gods" are also trying to go up to a higher level so that they, too, can be closer to the real God.

Watch out when religions or spiritual teachers point you to anything less than the one real and true ultimate God. If I have a problem and ask the President of the United States to help me, even though he is a powerful and exalted figurehead, it's still very different than if I seek the original God to help. But we get so impatient or feel we are unworthy, so we are tempted to seek help from lower levels rather then press on toward the true God.

You need to constantly work toward cleaning and purifying your energy so that you are not fooled by all the noise from both this human dimension and the other spiritual dimensions. That's why many of those great religions originally tried to tell you to worship only the real God. They tried to point the right way so that you wouldn't get confused.

The safest way to not get fooled and to make the most progress is to keep you heart, mind and soul fixed on the one true God. Even though you will brush up against the spiritual dimension in your journey, know that you already have everything you need inside of you to make it.

Remember that human beings have a piece of that original God inside — our Te. That Te is like a tunnel that can take you directly back to that one true God. That is why the best practice focuses on connecting with that Te inside you, not connecting to anything else "out there."

In my novel about the *Tao Te Ching* called *Nine Nights with the Taoist Master*, a monk comes to ask Lao Tzu why his prayers never work. Lao Tzu tells him it is because he is praying in the wrong direction. Whenever we look outside and outward in our effort to reach God, we can get easily confused and blocked by that spiritual dimension. That's why the real priority for those who want to reach Tao is to aim your meditation and prayer inward, trying to connect to that Te inside. Then that Te can carry your prayer to God, bypassing all that interference out there in the spiritual dimension.

So-Called "Good" Energy and "Bad" Energy

What we call evil and what we call angels are both the offspring of God. It's just a matter of which direction those spiritual energies are heading. Are they heading in the direction of return to the life and truth of God? Or are they heading away from the life and truth and God?

In God's universe nothing is wasted. Everything has a purpose and a job to do at whatever stage of the journey it's in. Evil has a purpose and a job too. Are you surprised?

When you see lions go out to kill and eat, they're just doing their job. Bacteria eating away at dead tissue are just doing their job. Predators and scavengers are very necessary in nature. Without them, our planet would be a mess. You cannot say bacteria or lions are "evil." They're just doing their job. We are the ones that turn our noses up at what they do and label it as "evil."

That destructive side of power is equal to the nourishing power in our universe. Remember how we said the sun couldn't function if it didn't have both gravity pulling in and heat and light radiating out? Balance requires both sides of the coin. That includes the nourishing and destructive power in our universe.

God, the Origin of the universe, expresses itself through both powers – Yin and Yang. They are both the same energy of God; it depends on how that energy flows. Good and evil both use God's power. The difference is whether that power is used for destruction or whether it's used for nourishing and healing.

Does this mean we live in a dualistic world of two equal powers constantly battling or revolving around each other? Not exactly. There is always the activity of Yin and Yang, evil and angel. But in the Center of it all is one true God who is greater than both of these powers because it is the one substance of both. So there is really only One. The fact that we see God's energy moving in two directions fools some into thinking that God is a two-faced God, or there is some battle raging all the time between a God and a Devil. It's not really that way.

Both powers come from the same God, and both are always together. You cannot have Yin without Yang, inward without outward. It's impossible. There are always both in every situation.

The true one God has the ultimate character of mercy, nourishing, kindness, and creativity. But sometimes, in order to create, something must be destroyed. You have to tear down a mistake to build something better. Old cells must die to be replenished with fresh new cells. Old plants must rot and decay to make fertile soil for new plants. Tao only destroys to build something better, to benefit and nourish all of creation, to keep everything in balance.

Tao is always exercising Yin and Yang, and as such our universe is always changing — always alternating between decay and renewal. Can you look throughout this universe and think of any exception? Even the stars are slowly dying, while at the same time far away nebulae are birthing new stars. Everything is in one of three states at all times: before change, during change and after change. Even our earth that seems so stable to us is constantly changing.

Given the constant change in the universe and in our lives, the constant decay and renewal, the constant motion of all parts of creation either toward or away from God, what's the difference between so-called "good" energy, and "bad" energy?

The difference is more a matter of how God's action of nourishing or destruction feels to us at the time. Do we like it or don't we like it?

For a moment, let's pretend God's energy is like sound. Sound can take on many different purposes and forms. We enjoy some sounds and dislike other sounds. Sound can be pleasant to us, like a symphony, or noisy like a jackhammer.

With such a wide range of sounds, only a very narrow range of sound falls into the category of what we accept as great music. Outside that range is what we might think of as bad music. Further outside that range is what we label "noise." Even further out of that range is harmful damaging noise like a firecracker exploding next to your ear or a jet engine at take-off. All of these come from the same energy called sound. The question of whether it is good or bad sound relies on what effect it has on us.

Light is like that too. If it's too bright, it hurts our eyes and can even blind us. If it's too dim, we cannot see. There's a narrow range of light that is good for us and useful to us.

Like light or sound, spiritual energy that is nourishing and harmonious to us fits within a range of what we call "good energy". Good energy is wonderful to us, just like good music. Any energy outside of that range is noisy, polluting or disrupting to us — meaning "bad energy."

Everybody wants to stay in that 72 degree comfort zone. Nobody wants to be in a room that's super-hot or super-cold. But how can we stay in that range of God's energy that is comfortable and nourishing to us? We have to work for it and we have to protect it.

People think "Well if *all* energy comes from God then it doesn't matter if I surround myself with good energy or evil energy. It's all the same if it's all from God." The trouble is that if you choose to surround yourself with evil energy, you risk picking up that vibration and making it part of your energy. Evil energy is part of God, but its heading in the direction of moving out and away from the Center. If you grab onto bad energy in your life, your own energy and direction can be turned away from God and you, too, could start heading away from the Center.

Moving away from God means more limitation, more suffering, and more destruction. Remember, in the end all things eventually return to God, so moving away doesn't mean you'll stay away from God forever. You'll just suffer that much longer. Do you really want to do that?

On the other hand, if you can surround yourself with good energy that helps straighten your direction and point you back toward God, you can travel closer to the Center.

We Are Made From Recycled Energy

While all this energy is coming and going, swirling and churning, to and from God, we are right in it. That soup is all around us. All those energies are moving around and through our dimension, whether or not we realize it. They're right here while you are reading this book.

Some people can see or feel or interpret these other dimensions. In fact, that's what real feng shui is all about. Feng shui isn't changing your wallpaper or moving furniture around to improve your luck. Feng shui is also not about you controlling where energy flows, as if you can steer it around based on your own human desires. Real feng shui is when you can raise your energy high enough to see how other spiritual dimensions are overlaid on ours, and you can decide how to best take advantage or cope with what is going on in those spiritual dimensions.

For example, we might build a tall building right in the middle of a spiritual highway where the spirit world likes to travel back and forth. That's very insulting to those beings in that spiritual dimension. If you continue to build there, they might try to get even with you in the future and hurt your business affairs. A real feng shui master can see that and help you avoid that mistake.

Energy from those different spiritual dimensions, that "soup," can affect us even before we are born. The spark of life in our first single cell is that piece of God called Te inside us. Even before our physical conception, our Te brought with it the residue of all the spiritual layers and "soup" that it traveled through on its own journey from the heart of God into this dimension.

That time between our conception and birth seems irrelevant to us now. But for that single cell to travel through those ten months of slow and painstaking work to become an embryo, then a fetus and then a baby, was like an epic undertaking of many eons from its perspective. It was a miraculous feat to grow from one single cell into the many trillions that we are made of today. Talk about a journey of 10,000 miles!

While you were growing inside your mother's womb, you had to gather proteins, enzymes, minerals and Chi to create your body, your organs, your brain, your tissue. You didn't multiply from one into a trillion living cells without bringing in building material.

But the tricky thing is that all the ingredients you pulled in to build yourself were used before by something or somebody else. Just like a drop of water you drink today may have been drunk by Queen Victoria long ago, the protein that your embryo brought in to make your liver could have been used before by a cow that became the hamburger your mother ate for lunch. Likewise, the human life energy, or Chi, that we pulled in to coat us and help us build and enliven our bodies is also recycled. It was used before by others. Because it was used before, it carries an imprint, a signal that then becomes a part of you too.

Everybody comes into this life coated with various layers of recycled energy. This miraculous process creates the unique individual you are today. It's one of the reasons no two people are alike. No person has the exact combination of recycled parts and uniquely imprinted energy that you do.

It also explains some of the different interests and urges people have. If I borrowed Chi that once was used by a doctor, as I grow up I might find that the field of medicine really appeals to me. It somehow makes sense to me. If I have Chi that was once used by a banker, I may discover that I really enjoy counting money and I find myself thinking of profits and financial deals all day long.

But being built from energy and materials that have been used before creates a problem. Some of the many energies used to make "you" may have strong negative signals or defects that also become part of you. You may have energy that was used by a thief. You wonder why you have a hard time controlling your urge to take things. You can have energy used by somebody else that hurt many people in another life, and now you have many enemies in this life but don't know why.

But we aren't just coated with recycled human energy; we can even be coated by energy from those different levels of the material and spiritual dimensions. Our Te might have a coating we brought in from a high angelic or "good" spiritual layer. Or, we might even have energy inside us that is more like evil.

What's even more confusing is that most people have many, many layers or coatings of used, borrowed, recycled energy from many of these different levels all at the same time. It takes a lot of energy to create a human being, so you pulled in whatever you could while you were forming that embryo. Whatever part of the universe our world was traveling through, whatever energy was flowing through your mother that day, whatever was traveling through that energy "soup" on the day you needed to make a lung, or a kidney or your brain, you took it in. You had to! Even if the material was dirty or not the best, if you needed it, you had to take it.

Just like if we are traveling from New York to California, at some point we get hungry and have to stop for food. If there's a nice restaurant with healthy and well-prepared food, great! But if all we see for miles and miles are dirty, greasy hot dog joints, then that's what we'll be forced to eat. We have no choice. We'll take in those hot dogs.

Unfortunately, when we decide we want to improve our lives and head back to God, we find out that all those coatings, those recycled pieces of energy, hold us back. There may be defects leftover in that energy that distorts our frequency. Those distortions can point us in the wrong direction or even drown out that frequency of God we are looking for. If we have Chi that was once used by a thief, it might be very hard to turn that energy toward God and away from stealing. On the other hand, sometimes those coatings can help. If we have Chi that was once used by a monk, it may be much easier for us to create a spiritual lifestyle and make better choices.

Those old signals, those defects, are what some teachings refer to as "karma," debt, or sin. This is part of what stands in our way and prevents us from touching the real God. That is why a big part of the spiritual journey is cleaning up our energy to get rid of those leftover defects. We have to fix it. It doesn't seem fair, but that's the price we pay when we borrow that energy.

Until we can clean up and repair our life energy, we are trapped in this human dimension. It's time to talk about that dimension and why we suffer so much while we are here.

PART THREE:

Who Are We?

道

We are Limited by False Understanding

How can we be in the network of God, have a piece of God inside of us, but at the same time get so far away from that original power of God? If everything is part of God, how did our human world get so confused and troubled? How have we remained so limited, ignorant and blind?

Let's look at our condition. After all, if we are going to explore what God is and the spiritual dimension, then we must also ask the question, "Who are we?"

As human beings, we have a piece of God's energy trapped in a very limited dimension. That is why we suffer.

God's energy is super-intelligence and super-creativity. Its thinking is so powerful, strong and big, and we are right in it. We are part of it and have a piece of it inside of us. But since we are trapped in such a limited dimension, our thinking is no longer "complete" thinking. We are limited. When we try to understand or solve a problem, we use our limited abilities and limited ways of thinking. That's why we can't really solve anything in the end, and we continue to suffer.

Our thinking is so limited, non-direct, unclean and so far from original truth, that it leads to very artificial ways of understanding things. These artificial and wrong ideas turn around to trap us even more deeply inside this wrong dimension. We have so many wrong ideas. We continually build new wrong ideas on top of our old wrong ideas. Our whole understanding of ourselves and our world is fake on top of fake on top of fake and more fake.

What are some examples of artificial thinking and fakeness? There are many. Language is fake because we made it up in order to communicate. Money is fake because we made it up in order to make our lives more convenient. Even your name is just an idea somebody had and then placed on you to make it convenient for everyone else to identify you.

But how are these examples fake and not real? Although we use these things every day, they are all just *concepts* that we agree on, not necessarily truth.

Today a dollar buys a candy bar, but tomorrow we might wake up and find that the whole world now believes that the dollar is worthless. We then need a thousand dollars to buy the same candy bar. So what is the truth about a dollar?

Or I believe the world is flat based on the flat horizon that I can see with my own eyes. I teach others the same "truth" and base entire religious laws and scientific schools on that "fact."

Artificial thinking and fakeness in our world are those things that we create or assume in our minds and then treat as if they were real.

Each time we revert to fake ideas, the frequency of our mind is reduced in tremendous proportion. As soon as you deal in fakeness, your power of mind drops exponentially and drops quickly.

On the other hand, true belief or faith is where the mind gets real. When you can break out of your cocoon of fake thinking, then your mind waves get very powerful. Then you can use the pure real power of your own mind to connect back to the original God and God's power. But the vast majority of people cannot do this.

Our Broken Connection to God
So what exactly separates us from God? What is the reason for our fake thinking? Well, part of the reason is due to that "recycled energy" we are made of. The defects in our energy distort God's signal to us and give us wrong ideas and wrong thoughts.

The problem is that we believe those wrong ideas and wrong thoughts and follow them. We think they are "our thoughts" or "our ideas," when they may simply be an echo of an old distorted frequency. Those distorted frequencies turn us away from God's way, and make us think we have the right answers.

The result is that we continue to choose to figure out our own problems with our own distorted mind and our own limited power, instead of relying on God's mind and God's power.

You see, we were originally created to receive and respond to God's frequency. But we changed the dial.

Did you ever wonder what Lao Tzu meant in the *Tao Te Ching* when he said that *"Tao treats everything as if it were a sacrifice"*? Many people are puzzled by this statement. It seems so depressing and strange. How and why are we all like sacrifices?

We are like a sacrifice because we are originally created to be characters in the Creator's drama. We were supposed to instantaneously respond to God's will. We are supposed to function as players in that giant screenplay that is created in the universal mind of God.

We were designed to function with instant communication and oneness with God, much like that old story about the Garden of Eden. The Garden of Eden was considered a paradise. In that paradise Adam and Eve had no need for artificial systems like language or currency or government. They could instantly communicate with God and each other with no words. Everything they needed was supplied by God. There was no such thing as suffering. They were innocent, with no self-doubt or shame. They didn't even know they were naked. They moved and lived spontaneously in full contentment.

Just like the Garden of Eden, everything in our world was originally designed to unfold perfectly and naturally, and to run smoothly and harmoniously forever. How did this ideal creation get so complicated? How was this harmony abruptly derailed? It went off-track because we human players got "smart." We started to have ideas that we could create a better harmony of our own, outside of God's harmony. We forgot that we were part of God's power. Instead, we incorrectly thought we possessed this power independently on our own.

When we started to think and act independently, we detached from the feeling of oneness and connectedness to God's power. We decided to create our own dreams, instead of living within the dream of God. We humans broke away from the script and started to create our own "plays" within the master screenplay.

Can you imagine watching an award-winning Broadway show, and suddenly a few actors decide they don't like that show anymore? They decide to create a new script inside the original play, because they've determined that they would like something different than what the original playwright had in mind. It would be chaos on stage.

When we started to create our own agendas, our own "plays" within the master play, everything started to run downhill. Things were not smooth and perfect anymore. By chasing our own smart ideas in favor of listening and following the original intention of God, we forged a path that led away from harmony, away from connection and toward separation and suffering. We departed from the ultimate balance created by Tao.

It's as if God designed everything in the universe to run like a well-managed and profitable corporation. We, however, were unwilling to go along as employees of our original CEO. We decided it would be better to leave the corporation and go out on our own to open our own convenience stores and pawn shops.

After we later ran our own little businesses into the ground, we cried "Why God?" But it was never God's fault. We were the ones who left and moved away from God.

God created a "no problem way" for us, but we are now on our own. We separated from the universal dream of God looking for something better only to find that the self-directed life we chose has become a nightmare. It's a nightmare because we keep trying to recreate heaven or a "Garden of Eden" and we can't. The more we try, the worse our world seems to get.

Humans Keep Trying to Create Heaven
Deep inside we have a vague memory of what life should and could be – how it was when we were one with God.

That's part of our suffering. We're smart enough to know something is wrong with our human lives and our human world. That vague memory, that feeling that something is not right, makes us strive to improve our world and try to end this suffering inside and the suffering all around us. We want so badly to mimic God's way. We want to restore harmony and unlimited life and health, ever-renewing resources, and boundless capabilities. We want to recapture what we had when we enjoyed an uninterrupted connection to our God. We're trying so hard to make that "return" back to heaven by creating it here in our human world.

We separated from God's qualities of eternity, immortality and the power to instantly materialize what we need. So we race to find substitutes. After we dropped down to this limited state, we lost our ability to instantaneously communicate, so we created language to substitute for our severed connection to God and each other. We were no longer in harmony with the earth, so we had to hunt and create farms, laboring hard in order to feed ourselves. Human history is a saga of mankind grasping at artificial solutions to the suffering and problems that he himself created by leaving God's truth and God's will.

What's worse is that we use the same thing that caused our problem to try and fix it – our reliance on our own mind. That's why each vain attempt man uses to fix his suffering causes even more artificial problems. All of his solutions are artificial and draw him further from Tao, which creates more suffering, requiring more man-made solutions, and on and on and on.

We continue to extend this sorry and endless saga of problems and fake solutions today. Just pick up any newspaper or look out your window and see for yourself. Every answer we think we find to a problem only causes more problems. Take our health. Our hard and unnatural lives make our bodies wear down and cause our health to fail. What do we do? We create hospitals. After our hospitals grow and become more sophisticated, soon greed and corruption invade the medical establishment. Eventually basic health care is unaffordable for many, so we need health insurance and must write many laws to solve problems in our health care system. Those laws cause political problems and arguments and split people apart. In the meantime, has our health improved at all? Not much. We work and struggle to restore health for ourselves, but always and ultimately fail because after all of our efforts toward better health, we still die in the end.

We've lived apart from God for so long that we have been taught to accept that it is natural for us to age, grow ill and die. We are not supposed to age, grow ill and die. Did you know that?

Instead, we work hard not to get sick. We work hard not to age. We try creams, vitamin potions and even surgery in order to stay young. We even try to create a solution for the problem of death. We create life insurance! Does life insurance protect life? Of course not.

We constantly look for fake solutions to resolve fake problems. We are trained to take care of problems in an artificial way all of our lives. When you get in a car accident, your first thought is "insurance." Or when you get sick, you think "hospital," or once again, "insurance." Nobody thinks to ask "How did I get sick? Do I have to get sick?"

We never stop to ask ourselves as Buddha did, "Why are we born, why do we age, why do we suffer illness, why do we die?" We are not supposed to endure aging, illness and death. But we have been deceived and tricked into an artificial world where we accept these as immutable facts.

Instead of that carefree reliance on God, now we not only grow old, we have to worry if we'll even be able to survive when we are elderly. This world teaches us to fear our old age, otherwise they couldn't sell us even more insurance or sell us nursing homes and "assisted living." These fake ideas that we embrace are just pollution in our minds. Fake built upon fake. If we were completely connected to God we would never grow old in the first place. Our lives would be eternal. All those problems with insurance and assisted living would seem silly.

Yet we aren't connected to God, so we keep trying to create our own heaven. We create an education system to fix our ignorance, a banking system to give us the illusion of security and prosperity, laws to curb wrong-thinking and wrong-doing, endless material goods to provide comfort and entertainment, advertisement to convince us that we should desire Hollywood's illusion of success and status.

In the end, none of it satisfies us. None of it fixes our problems. We remain without enlightenment, without security, without peace, and without a true sense of our purpose or worth. Once again, all of these human institutions are just our pitiful efforts to restore the harmony we enjoyed effortlessly when we were in connection to God. When one lie is initiated, many lies follow. We are on a treadmill and it seems we cannot get off.

When we play God's role by thinking we are smart and can "fix" something better than God can, we commit a serious offense. But we do it all the time. We tamper with nature, create some new contraption to change the world, create math, create science, and try to solve something we see as a problem. In thousands of ways, day in and day out, we try to create our own illustrious human heaven.

When we create an artificial system to solve our problems, not only do we separate ourselves further from God, we open a way for evil thinking to seep in. If you are tightly connected to God, there is no room for evil to come in. But in an artificial system, in a polluted mind, in a limited dimension cut-off from oneness with God, it is easy for evil to find a way to invade.

Evil is simply that energy which is heading *away* from God. Evil thinking is thinking that is opposite to the natural truth and God's way of thinking. Such evil thinking can and has infiltrated every artificial system in our world.

Conditions in our world have gotten so bad now that it's hard for anyone to deny we've gone far off-balance. Look at our environment, our social structures, our wars, our economic conditions. Evil thinking and wrong intentions take over the controls and then what do we do? We scramble around for more complicated and artificial solutions, but as a result, we create more ways for evil thinking to come in.

All these huge artificial systems start with one idea in one person's mind. Communism started as one idea of a man named Karl Marx. He just had one amazing idea. The idea in and of itself sounded pretty good, didn't it? But because it was an artificial solution, evil thinking easily took over and many millions died because of his one idea. That's why if I want to find the real truth, I have no "ideas"— I just connect to God.

But instead of letting go of their ideas, human beings have built a hell-like structure and cannot get out. The challenge is to break through the gates of this artificial world and find a way to restore the real connection that we were meant to enjoy.

The only way out is to spiritually wake up. The answer is to connect back to that Source. It requires hard work, but there is a way. If you do not, you are on your own and are doomed to continue in this limited, problem-filled dimension as the majority of people have throughout history.

The World Keeps You Busy and Keeps you From God
This fake world not only separates us from God, it steals our energy. As our human institutions and artificial ideas pile higher and higher, they swallow all of our attention and life force as we struggle to maintain them. Remember how God told Adam and Eve when they left the Garden of Eden, "You will work hard!" And indeed we do.

To be successful in our world means to be occupied by endless artificial demands. We are so busy with the complications of our daily lives, we have no time or energy left to feel God.

Some people, like the Amish, try to protect themselves from so many crazy artificial man-made systems. The elders who advised the Amish to preserve their way of life most likely realized that man-made systems not only increase our separation from God, but distract us from seeking and relying on God. So their idea was to adopt a simple technology-free way of life.

A group of students and I visited an Amish family one time to learn more about their lifestyle. One student asked them, "What do you do for fun?" They looked at us and wondered why anyone would ask such a strange question. They didn't realize there was any need for separating activities between work and fun, or worship and fun, or that there was some type of human need for fun. And yet they certainly weren't cheerless. On the contrary, everything they did throughout their day, they did in a spirit of worship and closeness to God, so they were generally peaceful and happy all day long. They never had a sense that they suffered from a lack of fun, or needed complicated equipment and activities for "fun" the way people in more modern lifestyles do.

When people need entertainment or are "bored," it indicates they have a cavity inside. When they are uncomfortable and worried about how to spend their time, it indicates they are very far from their original selves. Their search to alleviate boredom invites fake things to move in and fill up that cavity. Those things are usually the sort that will pull them even further away from their original selves. What they reach out for to pass the time, to distract themselves, usually has a bad message and creates even more problems. That distraction, and the need for distraction, pulls you away from God.

Old kings and their governments knew that distractions keep people away from God. That's why they always had a big project underway to keep everyone busy: build this Great Wall, construct this huge city temple, or go to war. If you weren't forced to help work on the project, you were forced to work even harder to pay the taxes to finance them. The old kings knew the benefits of keeping people focused on such distractions. It kept the people well-controlled and kept the wheels of profit rolling.

The only way to worship God is if you have a simple lifestyle: one where you aren't consumed by demands and constant distractions. I'm not advising everyone to become like the Amish. I am saying that you need to be detached enough from the artificial systems around you so that they do not occupy your mind. Why? You need to be free enough to be able to focus your mind on God, not on artificial things. If you have 1,000 things to worry about, will you have time to meditate and cultivate the peaceful pure mind necessary to connect and listen to God? No.

Here's an example of how our world and it's values can occupy you so much, it can completely consume your time and energy: In our world, people worship money first and then job titles and degrees. (The main reason people worship titles and degrees is because they know that titles and degrees mean better pay.) Nowadays, for most people, it is too expensive to attend a university. Why? Because everybody knows you need a good degree to make more money, so universities know they can charge more money to get that degree. So families have to mortgage their house and work two jobs just to afford a college degree for their child so that he or she can make more money in the future. Yet titles, degrees and currency are all manmade and fake. But this fakeness has taken over the lives of many of today's families.

The business of this world and its artificial system requires you to be very busy and also requires you to have lots of troubles. The systems in our society thrive on trouble. Imagine if nobody got sick? There would be no more doctors, hospitals, pharmaceutical companies or health insurance. That huge system depends on everyone to get sick in order to keep its sector of the economy going.

Imagine if there was no crime. We wouldn't need policemen, lawyers, courts and prisons anymore. Another huge chunk of our economy would disappear. If we had no car accidents, we wouldn't need auto insurance, disability insurance, or personal injury lawyers.

This whole dead-end human world thrives on distraction, trouble and keeping you enslaved to its artificial solutions. It thrives on draining your energy. It is very difficult to create a lifestyle that still has room for the type of practice and sincerity necessary to reconnect with God.

The Dead Treat Everything as if it Were Dead

Separated from the original harmonious energy of God, we are no longer in our right mind. Individually and collectively, we behave as if we are mentally ill.

Look at our environment. Most people say that we have an environmental problem today. However, at the root, it is a mental problem, not an environmental problem. Only those who are separated from God, who see everything around them as dead and disconnected, would venture to throw poisons into the air that they themselves must breathe, or into the water that they themselves must drink.

What if we restored our minds and saw the truth that the whole universe is alive and permeated with God and connected together as one piece? That we humans are also connected to God and that each of our thoughts and actions do indeed matter and impact the whole? Then we would no longer be mentally ill. We would need no laws to protect the environment, because nobody would dream of polluting. It would run against our very nature.

There is an old saying that the mentally ill suffer twice. What does this mean? It means that those with mental illness not only suffer mentally, but suffer physically as well. A person who is mentally ill often neglects their health, eats a nutritionally poor diet, or neglects basic safety measures in their daily life. They often suffer from physical injury, homelessness, exposure to heat and cold, assault and illness because they are incapable of taking care of themselves in the proper way. So they suffer both in mind and in body.

This is the state of our whole world today. Just like the mentally ill, we suffer twice. Inside we suffer the pain and disorientation of separation from God, and outside we suffer from the physical damage we do to ourselves, each other and the world as a result of our damaged minds.

To the degree that we cannot feel that original life energy inside of us, then we are dead to that same degree. If we are dead and out of touch with our own life energy, we see other things and treat other things like they are dead. We kill and trash everything around us, like we trash the air, the water, animals and the planet.

Those who are dead inside want other people around them to act and feel dead inside too, because it makes them feel more comfortable. They are not satisfied until everyone around them embraces the same artificial and fake ideas and systems that all the other walking dead embrace. They are so invested in you being dead like them, they will work to make you miserable until you conform.

The reason they do this is that being dead inside makes you feel insecure. The reason we care so much about what other people think is because we are dead inside. We use an outside artificial reference, because we have no connection to our own life energy. Our "self" becomes the accumulation of recognition from outside, not our True Self which is that piece of God inside of us. However, when we wake up our awareness of life energy we treat things differently. We don't care what others think anymore. It's irrelevant because our own true signal is so strong.

When you start the journey toward rediscovering the original energy inside you, you start heading a different direction than the walking dead around you. But because you are swimming against that human current, you will feel different and alone sometimes. This is why Lao Tzu talks about how other people seem so busy and caught up with distractions, while he feels like an outsider:

> *"I fear what everyone else fears."*
> *So long this has been such a pointless idea.*
> *I wonder when it will stop.*
> *Everyone else is indulging themselves,*
> *as if enjoying the sacrificial feast of the ox.*
> *As if in spring some enjoy climbing the terrace at the park.*
> *I alone seem unaffected and lost,*
> *Like an innocent baby that hasn't yet learned to smile*
> *I alone have no place to go*
> *Others have more than enough, but I alone am lacking.*
> *I feel like a fool, as if I were confounded.*
> *Everyone else appears bright, but I alone am dim.*
> *Everyone else appears to be so smart,*
> *but I am the only one who is confused....*
> *Everyone else acts capable,*
> *but I'm the only one who acts stubborn and foolish.*
> *I am different, but I am nourished by the great mother."*
>   Lao Tzu, *Tao Te Ching*, Chapter 20

When Lao Tzu says "I alone," he's not talking about the type of loneliness we feel at the human level. Our everyday feelings of loneliness happen because we are cut off from our own original energy, so we try to fill it up with outside things. In contrast, Lao

Tzu values his emptiness and solitude. The words of Lao Tzu are telling you: Don't fill your mind up with other artificial things and outside distractions like terraces at the park or sacrificial feasts of the ox. By staying empty and detached from the busy activities of the artificial world, you can make that real connection and fill up with the true signal of your original energy. That way you too can be nourished by the "great mother" — meaning God.

Passion Versus Profit: How Good Systems Get Hijacked

We humans are busy running around creating solutions to our problems by inventing new systems. Not all of those systems start out bad, or are bad intentioned. They simply get hijacked by those with wrong intentions or evil thinking.

For example, hospitals aren't a bad idea. Helping sick people is not wrong. Hospitals started out as charitable endeavors, usually staffed by monks or nuns devoted to helping relieve the suffering of the sick as a service to God. Those working in hospitals did so out of a sincere heart. But over time, the hospitals were gradually taken over by business enterprises that now run them for profit. The "bottom line," not charity, became the new priority in the hospital world. Prices went up while the nuns and monks were replaced with professionally trained staff requiring higher salaries. Malpractice suits loomed, so the hospital needed risk managers and extra testing done on each patient to be sure there were fewer lawsuits. Over time, the system has become so complex that it could very well break down. Do you see how a good idea got hijacked over time by wrong motives seeping in?

Let's look at money. Many religious people like to claim "Money is evil." Money isn't bad. Money, as currency, started out as a very good idea. It makes trade easier. If I'm a fisherman and you grow apples, I can give you some of my fish for some of your apples. But if you don't need any of my fish today, I need something I can give you in order to get the apples I want. So we agree to trade little pieces of silver or gold or polished clamshells with each other, so that everybody can get what they need, when they need it, in the marketplace. Good idea!

Then along comes somebody calling themselves a "banker." They offer a safe place to store your extra gold or clamshells so that nobody will steal them and you don't have to carry them around all day. Okay. This is a little more complicated, but still not necessarily a bad idea.

Then bankers get the idea to loan the money they are watching for you out to new merchants at a rate of interest. Pretty soon they loan out more and more in order to make a profit. See how the system is getting more complicated?

Centuries later, we now have bond markets, stocks, commodities, a thousand different types of loans and derivatives, and even money itself has become mere blips on a computer screen. People have to study for years to earn a degree in economics just to understand, or pretend to understand, how it all works. Along the way, greedy people have invaded this complicated money system in several different places, corrupting the way it works in order to make a profit at the expense of others. It's easy for them to do, because the system is so complicated that nobody can even understand it anymore, much less notice where and how evil thinking has hijacked the system.

The profit motive is one of the main reasons our best artificial systems get hijacked by evil. And as we layer more artificial solutions, more complications, we create more opportunities for wrong thinking and "evil" to slip in.

What's the difference between evil and angel? The energy that's working on trying to go back to God is the angel. The energy that is disconnected from, traveling away from, acting on its own despite of, staying away from, or working to deny God is evil.

Everything I'm doing without respect to original nature is evil. For example: People have a passion to watch birds. They naturally delight in it. Is there anything wrong with that? No! But now I've decided to hijack the system so only rich people can afford to watch birds. I've fenced off all the sanctuaries, charge a high admission, require fancy clothes and equipment to get in, and lured all the birds to my sanctuaries by cutting off their food everywhere else. That's evil. That's not a service any more. That's not a passion. That's done for profit.

A "passion" is from original nature. "Profit" is opposite from passion. It's the sincere and real versus what is fake. Passion means you do something at any cost with no care about the return. Profit means you do things for a purpose or to gain something. Manipulating an existing system, or unfairly exploiting people's natural wants and needs for profit, like our bird-watching example, is "non-God."

Why do we have such a huge population on our planet? Those who thrive on artificial systems love more population, because they love profit. More people mean more slaves to my artificial system and more profit — that is if I manipulate it just right. The artificial systems that run our planet today thrive on continued growth. It doesn't matter if a population of 10 billion people will kill the planet twenty years from now, investors want and need profit today, or our whole economic system will collapse.

From the time we are born the world teaches us that when we do anything we should have a purpose or a profit in mind. "Give to charity, but don't forget the tax write-off!" "Eat your peas, and then you can have dessert." "Be good and when you die you'll go to heaven!" We do good things only for benefit — expecting some reward. We never learn that there is more than this. We never know there is a higher level, a better way to be.

Profit has squeezed into this system so much that most of the time you cannot honor your passion and survive. For example, a true chef should never own a restaurant. A chef cares about the quality and source of her ingredients. She cares about the health and enjoyment of those that eat her food. Cooking to the chef is an art, an activity that brings joy and is done from a true heart.

To make a profit in the restaurant business is different than being a chef. If a restaurant owner really wants to make a profit, she will load up the food with fat, sugar and salt because people are built by nature to crave fat, sugar and salt for survival. Then she will hunt around for the cheapest source of ingredients so that her profit margin is bigger. It doesn't matter where the ingredients come from or how unethically they are manufactured. They're cheap! Then when the profits start to roll in, she will franchise her restaurant system into a thousand corner fast-food joints where people can slurp up the fat, sugar and salt, regardless of how it affects their health.

Working from passion is completely different. The Wright brothers owned a simple little bike shop on the coast of North Carolina. Their passion was flying. They tinkered and played, motivated by nothing but that fascination and passion. They invented human air travel. Look at where air travel has come today. Now the Wright brothers never enjoyed much profit out of that invention, even though the air industry now earns trillions of dollars. Their amazing discovery and gift to the world came out of passion, not profit.

Thomas Edison also worked from passion. One night his barn caught on fire. This was no ordinary barn. It was the barn where all of his inventions were stored and where he worked. When he saw the flames, he ran to the bedroom and grabbed his wife and said, "Honey, come take a look at this! You'll never see a fire like this again in your life." He was simply living in the moment, living from passion. He wasn't worried about his lost work or his lost profit.

People can even use morality, etiquette and religion for profit. I'm not just talking about the television ministers asking you to mail in money, or storefront preachers who skip town after the collection plate comes in. It is even more subtle than that.

There are people who appear very nice, but in actuality, they are trying to be good people for the sake of profit. They figure by being nice, they'll get something back from their neighbors, family, workmates or friends. Whether they are looking for respect, an increased chance of getting a favor someday, a better job, or hope that others around them will be nice in return, they count on their niceness to bring them a profit. In the long run, they are nicer to those who they figure they can get more out of and only a "little bit nice" to people who are useless to them. See how their niceness is for profit? Their niceness is fake.

It is not that profit is immoral or bad. The critical matter is that if I go along with the fakeness that accompanies a profit-based mind, I cannot reach the frequency I need to reconnect with God. It's sad when you see people try to bargain with God. Why do they do that? Because they've been raised to bargain all their lives, so they bring that type of bargaining approach to God. If you are profit minded and approach God with that type of bargaining attitude, you simply cannot make it. Your frequency will not match God's frequency.

Government and the Need for Freedom
Forms of government are like other ideas that start out good but then get hijacked. It's not a bad idea to group together and agree

to a few rules. Organizing together can help everyone in the community stay safe and prosper. But why does government usually evolve into a system full of trouble? Just like the financial system, government often grows into a highly complicated system that can be easily hijacked by wrong thinking and profit-mindedness.

Throughout the *Tao Te Ching*, Lao Tzu talks about government. He says the best governments are those that interfere with people the least. Why? Lao Tzu knew that if people are not distracted and controlled by government interference, they have more freedom. Freedom means personal independence. It means a life and mind that is "unoccupied." This is important because unless you have freedom, you cannot worship the true God.

If I force you, either by education or military power, to pledge your loyalty to king and country first, then you may be able to participate in a state-sanctioned religion, but you cannot worship the real God. In order to worship the real God, you must be totally free. If you are under the constant influence and mental pollution of outside control, then you will inevitably fail to reach the pure frequency necessary to reach the true original God.

In the old days, the old Tao wisdom could flourish because people could establish small temple-like communities far away from the world's activity. In fact, the old Taoists were called "mountain men" because they often lived off in the mountains, away from the busy villages and towns. The government didn't bother to go find them or tax them or force them to go to war. What the mountain men did or didn't do was irrelevant to most people in the town, because the mountain men lived so far outside of regular society and rarely came in contact with town folks. The seclusion of the mountain men's small groups allowed their minds to remain unoccupied by the world's artificial values or interpretations. They could better focus on their own internal energy and what was necessary for reconnecting to God.

The old Taoists also called themselves "real men" or "real women." The fact that they considered themselves "real" implied that the other people living in day-to-day human society were not real. The Taoists considered that living in society meant being occupied by the artificial ideas and activities that served to cut people off from their own original nature and the Tao.

One of the reasons that the old temple system collapsed is that as civilization grew, government control spread deeper and wider. It became harder and harder to operate outside of that government's influence and control. Whether they liked it or not, government affairs and politics started rubbing up closer and closer against the temples and spiritual communities. Eventually government influence and control seeped in. In the end, conflict erupted and many temples were torn down or burned to the ground by government armies.

Today, it is even worse. Where can you go to escape the tax collector, the draft board, the police department, the census bureau, the post office, the television news, the Internet, or any of our human society's long tentacles? It is virtually impossible.

Instead, we are forced to find ways to work toward a lifestyle where we can live within human society, but not be pulled into the fakeness of it to the point that it controls or occupies our minds. We must try to do as Jesus said: "Be in the world, but not of it."

That's also why Jesus said such things as "Give Caesar what is Caesar's, and give to God what belongs to God." There's no need to avoid or fight the system. Give it its dues and be done with it so that you can put your mind back on God. Find a way to live inside of it, but stay detached.

I keep saying to my students, "Simplify." Simplify means I'm not going to participate in the world's artificial systems. I'm going to "use" those systems when I have to, but I'm not going to be occupied or used by them.

What's the difference between simply using a system and being occupied or used by it? In today's day and age, you have to have a checking account or some cash in order to buy food. But that doesn't mean you have to become preoccupied with the financial system. You have to pay your taxes or you risk going to jail. So pay your taxes and forget about it. Let the empire do what evil or good it will do with its money, and in the meantime you return you energy and attention to God. Do what's minimally necessary to get along in the world system and keep it off your back, and reserve the rest of your life for God.

Simplifying also means to detach from those things people normally desire. When there's nothing you need or want, then nobody can manipulate and control you. If other people know what it is you want, then they will use that to control you.

Politicians and government officials know human nature. They know what people want and they can use that to exploit people. Just as those running the financial system know what people need and can exploit it. Whatever you want or need, they will promise you that very thing. Whatever you depend on, that will be what they hijack.

In today's world, you need money to do most anything. So they say, "If you need money, you have to borrow it from my corrupt system, because I control money." When you apply for a loan, you will have to give them all your personal information – your net worth, your social security number, names of your relatives. By doing this, when you come into the money system you now give up a certain amount of your freedom. You also become a source of profit for them, so they make sure you can never leave. You cannot get out, because you'll need another loan to buy a house, run a business or pay a doctor. You're trapped.

The financial system knows that it is natural for people to want their own house in order to raise a family. Knowing this, evil thinkers inside the financial and government systems can manipulate the housing market, making a profit from people's honest urge to get a house of their own. Instead of creating a fair and honest mortgage system, they can abuse the whole housing system nationwide for profit, with your full cooperation. What's more, for even more profit they can then crash that whole mortgage system, taking down the economy of the entire world in the process. Why? Is it because mortgages are bad? No. It's because evil thinking has hijacked that system.

Whatever you need and desire can be hijacked. If you desire success, somebody will find a way to manipulate and control your ability to succeed by taxes and laws that govern whatever business you are in. If you desire security, those systems will play on your fear and make you feel insecure in order to sell you insurance or a new investment fund. In the end, manipulation and control of what you need and want will always end up as profits for those that control those systems.

We were fated to suffer under such faulty human systems from the day we separated from God. Here's a simple example illustrating our condition: When we were with God we were never cold. But now that we're on our own without the warmth of God, we can feel the cold. It's cold, so we need clothes. To get clothes, we go out and kill animals and gather plant fibers to make clothes. One day somebody comes and takes my clothes. So I have to kill him to get my clothes back. Then we need laws to stop people from killing and laws to stop people from stealing clothes. Then we need courts, judges and lawyers to deal with those people we catch stealing clothes or killing. Then we need a prison to put them in. Then we need taxes to finance the prisons and courts and judges. People have to pay so many taxes, that they must go to work, and can't afford the time to hunt and weave for clothes anymore. So we buy our clothes from overseas where they use slaves to make clothes more cheaply. But now we need international trade agreements to import the slave-made clothes. We keep layering and inventing more solutions. Meanwhile, religion yells from the sidelines that it's immoral to be naked. You laugh, but this is how our world is today.

The fact that human systems evolve from good ideas, become corrupt and ultimately crash, is a pattern that can be seen throughout history over and over again. No empire or human system lasts forever. What's important to understand is that there's a dark force cooking these ideas, hijacking these systems and then manipulating things based on what you want.

This dark force even profits when its own systems collapse. Even if humanity suffers from natural disasters, accidents, tragic events, it is always profitable for them in the end. They have designed everything in advance to profit from whatever will happen in the future. That's why it is so difficult for us to find real solutions to our world's problems today. Those with evil and profit-motive thinking have invaded every solution and have anticipated every outcome.

Is the answer to dissolve governments and financial systems in order to prevent these dark forces from taking over? No. Civilization is a precious thing. We cannot regard civilization lightly or take it for granted as if we are entitled to it. Without the calm peacefulness of civilization, we would be far too busy trying to survive to worry about finding God.

But we have to find a way to balance the good in civilization while protecting ourselves from the profit-minded and evil influences that can come in and ultimately destroy it. Lao Tzu understood the vulnerability of civilization. He knew that if government had a limited role and was kept simple, the people would prosper. He knew that if government became complicated and over-bearing, it could be easily hijacked by evil thinking.

The founding fathers of the United States of America had a very spiritualized idea. They recognized the need for individual freedom, equality under God, and the right for people to pursue their own happiness. Those documents founding the United State were almost miraculous examples of clear spiritual thinking. *"We hold these truths to be self-evident..."* From the very beginning they acknowledge a higher truth not originating in the minds of men.

And that system they created eventually thrived for quite a long time. But like other good government systems of the past, over time it has grown more complicated and artificial. Profit-minded people with wrong interpretations and evil thinking keep finding their way into positions of influence and power.

What's worse, the general spirit of the people that valued individual liberty, trust, and the freedom to worship, the spirit that upheld a nation like the United States for so long, can be easily lost. That's why you see many examples in history of brilliant societies that rise and fall. The spirit of the people gets lost and evil thinking creeps in. You can look at ancient China, Japan, Greece and Rome and see brief spans of time where civilization was enlightened and compassionate, but then it quickly deteriorates again.

The sort of spirit in a nation that allows for trust, honest enterprise, creativity, personal freedoms, tolerance for differing opinions, and acknowledging higher truth is very precious. A nation can lose that spirit through evil thinking seeping in and taking over. And when that spirit is lost, it is almost impossible to regain.

What is a sign of deterioration in a civilization? When a society worships artificial and evil-minded ideas more than it respects honesty and freedom. Unfortunately, instead of trying to correct the evil and wrong thinking in our society today, we worship it. We reward those who steal, idolize those who lie, bail out companies who produce inferior products, and worship those who pursue money, fame and success at whatever cost. Compare how we worship the rich versus rewarding and praising those who do what is real and valuable to humankind. By our wrong thinking, we are putting this world even further out of balance and out of harmony with Tao.

Evil can escalate to such a high degree that the whole system of a nation can come crumbling down. That, too, serves evil. If we toss everybody into chaos, they don't have time to worship – and then their souls in turn go into decline. As a result of their decline things get even worse. We should be grateful for times of peace and calm, for those are the times when we can have the precious quiet and freedom we need to practice and meditate in our effort to reconnect with God.

The main reason governments grow ever larger and more complicated is that we still believe that laws and morals can help solve our problems.

Why Laws and Morals Can't Solve the Problem
Most people understand that to improve our world we have to correct our ways of wrong doing and wrong thinking. Collectively we may know and understand this, but why in human history have we been unable to correct much? Why do the same crimes, same wars, same greed, same bad ideas keep cropping up again and again, century after century?

The reason we can't correct the wrong thinking and bad behavior in our society, is because we use the wrong tools. For example, the main tool we use to try to correct people's wrong thinking and wrong doing is enacting laws and enforcing morals.

People, especially religious people, get very worried about moral issues. Moral issues are man-made issues. They are not God's issues. Moral issues are an example of man-made attempts to solve problems we ourselves have created. They cannot mend the separation between us and God.

Let's look at one of the many religious systems based on laws and morals. Confucius was a contemporary of Lao Tzu. They lived around the same time (approximately 500 B.C.) We know that

Confucius met and most likely studied under Lao Tzu because of several references he made to Lao Tzu and Lao Tzu's teaching of Tao in his life.

I always joke about Confucius being Lao Tzu's "failed" disciple. The biggest reason I poke fun at Confucius is because unlike Lao Tzu's teaching, Confucianism's teachings are full of "morals" and codes of behavior for every rank and function in society. Most of Confucius' morals concerned one's duty to family. His teachings were so popular, that many of his morals were adopted as law by Chinese society. There were laws requiring sons and daughters to be loyal to and respectful of their parents. There were laws governing right conduct in professional life. There were laws governing how people interacted with government.

It's not that Confucius' rules were bad. Most of them were very logical and, if implemented, would help society quite a bit. But Lao Tzu's teachings about morals are completely different. Lao Tzu says:

> "Renounce 'holiness' and give up 'wisdom,'
> and the people will benefit a hundred times over.
> Stop touting 'kindness,' throw away notions of 'morality,'
> and the people will be filled with fidelity and love.
> Give up cleverness, ignore the idea of profit,
> and there will be no more theft or robbery.
> These things only fix the surface; they are insufficient.

> *It is more important to help people embrace simplicity;*
> *To hold one's true nature;*
> *To restrain from being selfish and curtail desire."*
> Lao Tzu, *Tao Te Ching*, Chapter 19

Why does Lao Tzu tell us to throw away our morals? Because moral issues won't help us see God or feel God. Morals are man-made and do nothing to dissolve the pollution and defects in our energy that both cause our troubles and separate us from God. Since morals can't help you find your Te, they are irrelevant to the goal of connecting to God and thus a completely different thing than what we are talking about here in this book.

In fact, moral issues can be counterproductive, because people get side-tracked from their initial desire to try to connect to God. They end up spending so much effort focusing on morals, (which means nothing much more than practicing to be a socially correct person or a "nice guy") that they get distracted from the real goal — God.

Being a nice guy is wonderful, but it's not necessarily going to enable you to connect to God. For example, let's say I've worked very hard to be a nice guy with high moral standards. I'm forgetting one thing: the definition of "nice guy" relies on appearances and approval from others. It requires that many people all believe and agree with me that I'm a nice guy. My appearance of niceness must be approved by all the people around me, or I am not considered nice. And what the culture approves of in North America might be frowned on in the Middle East. What's nice in parts of Asia could be considered terrible in Europe. The approval of others varies from country to country because it isn't truth. Others are not God, nor does their approval reconnect us back to that original network.

This is why relying too heavily on morals is very dangerous. People try to be morally fit, but on a spiritual journey end up as total failures. Why? They neglect spending time to truly clean up their wrong doing and wrong thinking by eliminating the artificial pollution in their minds and restoring their original life energy. They've been too occupied learning what they have to do to be a good person to please other people out there who may be judging them. Their effort is going in the wrong direction. Our effort instead should be to burn off such artificial standards and thereby purify ourselves. You have to totally qualify yourself by changing your nature entirely, not by just acting moral.

Does this mean that we on a true spiritual journey behave like immoral or amoral people? Quite the opposite! If you can purify your mind and your life energy so well, then you naturally and effortlessly match up with the highest moral standard without even trying. You are so pure that you have no interest in wrong doing. But your pure conduct will be one that naturally unfolds from your connection to God, not by worrying about other people's standards or a list of moral rules.

Most laws and codes of moral behavior require force to maintain them. If you are in charge of managing society and your plan of keeping the peace depends on all people becoming pure and connecting with God, or even if you depend on a majority of people choosing to be morally fit nice guys, the odds of a peaceful and stable society are stacked against you. But if you bet on the power of force to demand that everybody adhere to the right behavior, you have a better chance.

Force, or likewise the church's threat of future punishment in hell, is necessary to back up moral codes and laws because inside many people still have a desire to do wrong things. What is inside people is the real problem, not how they act outside.

You cannot judge a person's spiritual condition only by how they behave on the outside. How can you tell whether someone is acting nice and moral because they are good and pure inside, or whether they're bad by nature and have simply been trained to act nice out of their fear of disapproval, punishment, jail, or hell? It is not their good nature, but the fear of punishment for moral violations that makes some people restrain from doing wrong.

On the other hand, if you are pure inside, it doesn't matter if the law is there or not, it doesn't matter if there are punishments or not, it doesn't even matter if there are no rewards for good behavior. When you are very pure, you naturally just don't want to do bad things.

Do you see the difference? The best situation is where you don't need laws to follow because you are so pure. The pure don't need laws or morals because they naturally feel what's right and what's wrong in every situation. But when you need the guideline of morals, the difference is that your buried desire, your natural inclination, is to do what the moral codes tell you not to do.

Poor Moses had to bring those Ten Commandments down from the mountain to say: "You shall not kill. You shall not steal." It is very bad that human civilization even came to that point. By your very nature, you should feel "I don't want to kill." No more than I wouldn't want to kill my own arms, my own cells. But if there's a law needed to tell me not to inject poison into my own arms or saw off my own legs, then I obviously have a big problem.

So if you need to have a law saying "Thou shall not steal," it's because you want something that doesn't belong to you or you need something because your life is so lacking. You also need a restriction on your behavior because you're not sure you can control yourself and your desires. This means your power is weak and you are already far away from God. If you are strong, you don't need or covet anything to begin with, and you don't need restrictions to enforce correct behavior.

If I keep myself close to God, and close to the way of nature, I don't need laws. I love my parents without even thinking about it and naturally would always treat them well. If there's a law saying you have to treat your parents nicely, like Confucius demands, this means people have already strayed far from truth.

Jesus understood the truth about morals and that they are inferior when compared to a natural connection to God. That's why he could summarize all the commandments into two: love

God with all your heart, and love your neighbor as yourself. That simple statement shows how Jesus knew that to be perfectly "moral" we must restore our oneness with God, and recognize that the entire universe and all people are part of God and thereby all connected. If we could manage those two things, we would naturally never do wrong.

Jesus also made another very interesting statement about morals. He said that if you even look at another man's wife with lust, it's the same as if you've committed adultery. This isn't a moral teaching. On the contrary, Jesus was describing the way God works. He knew that people could restrain themselves from doing bad things, but still have that same bad energy coating inside. The bad thoughts were the proof.

He also tried to say that the nothingness counts. He knew that there's a power flowing everywhere that comes from God that knows and registers everything. Even our silent thoughts and desires register on that network and echo in that transparent dimension, whether we realize it or not. And because of that, even if you act nice, lawful and moral on the outside in this physical world, you can't hide your true thoughts and intentions from God.

In this world, what people are thinking and feeling is hidden from us. So we cannot judge the truth about people by their moral behavior, because what they really hold in their minds and hearts could be something completely different. But in the dimension of God, nothing is hidden. That emptiness records all thoughts and intentions as well as actions. In that dimension the consequences for bad thoughts and bad actions are pretty much the same – you will fail to reconnect with God.

It's not whether what you think or do is moral or not, it's whether your mind is pure enough to match and reconnect with God's frequency. Remember the rule: if your energy is pure and light and matches the frequency of God you will get closer to that Center. If your energy is heavy and slow, you will fall further away. Bad actions will lower that frequency, but so will bad thoughts. This is because both spring from the same heavy, slow and negative energy inside of you. That's why Jesus said bad thoughts and actions were equal — because both keep you separated from God.

Religion's Big Mistake

Religions can make a big mistake when they treat God like a strict father figure or cruel judge who sets down rules and morals for this and for that. One religion's list of morals may be different from another religion's list of morals. The trouble is that God doesn't get involved in morals at all, per se. The real issue is your energy "frequency." Does it match up with God's frequency or not?

If your behavior is harmful, negative, artificial and evil, your energy will sink lower and you will fail to connect with God. If you are pure, natural, compassionate, humble and merciful, your energy will be lighter and more closely match God's frequency, making it more likely that you will be able to make that connection.

All of those religious teachings initially tried to guide people in the way back to God. They tried to help people raise their energy to establish a higher frequency that would give them a better chance to connect. They tried to show people how to sort out the bad messages from the good messages inside of them. But over time we turned those beautiful wisdom teachings into human level laws and "morals."

When you realize how God works, you realize: "I have to change myself and my energy deep inside in order to feel and to understand the real God, in order to truly 'pray' and connect." That's a totally different approach than today's interpretation of spiritual wisdom.

The cruelty of religion is that like any other man-made system, it can be taken over by wrong interpretations. That's why many religions end up telling you just to follow their rules and rituals, go to church once a week, say your prayers, give them money, and then you'll be right with God.

Religious institutions count on you to look to them for the answer. But we want to do more than that on our spiritual journey. We want to have the ability to connect directly with God for our answers. You can continue to be Catholic, Muslim, Buddhist or Hindu, but know that you can do better than simple rituals and mental beliefs. You can work toward a real connection with God in whatever religion or way of life you choose. By sharing Tao as the Way of God, this book is not telling you to quit being a Christian or a Jew or a Muslim. What it is saying is that by restoring your connection to God you can be an even better Christian, Jew or Muslim.

Likewise, there is no reason for Jews, Muslims or Christians to point fingers at each other in anger. That happens out of our polluted way of thinking. It is very easy to push the idea of hating different cultures to people rather than push the idea of our connection to each other. By our sinful, disconnected nature, we are easily annoyed by anything different. We fear and despise people who are different than us mainly because we are very insecure. Human beings have sin, meaning separation from their connection with God, so naturally they don't respect each other. They cannot comprehend or feel the power of the origin or Tao, for if they did, then they would naturally love each other.

If the God we are talking about is only the Russian people's God, then it's not God. Or if this is England's God, then it's not really God. If I know God, I would never insult Mormons, Buddhists, Sikhs, or anyone. But some religions kill each other, over what? If I think my God is better than your God, then it only proves that I'm worshipping the wrong God. In Genesis, how early did the first murder happen? It happened within the first generation after Adam left the Garden. The first murder happened after one brother became enraged with jealousy over another brother's different way of sacrificing to God. The first murder was a religious war.

Some religions talk about going to paradise when we die. If you cannot even take care of this planet and get along with each other, how can you get to paradise? Environmental, legal, societal and economic systems are starting to crumble down in every culture on this planet, and under every religious banner. So what does that say? It means we've all lost our way, and no religion has been able to stop our world's dead-end path.

I often wonder why those ancient prophets in every religion we know of, Islam, Christianity, Buddhism, had so much more spiritual wisdom and power than we do today. You never hear of people with the power of Moses parting the Red Sea anymore. Why not? Has our spiritual power as humankind grown even weaker with time?

We think we are smarter today than people were in those ancient times. We are pitifully mistaken. Without technology, without artificial "smarts," ancient people had to rely on their true feeling to learn. They used their imagination. They remained naïve and down to earth, relying on faith. Because of that, they were much closer to God's frequency. They were actually quite advanced in their ability to reconnect with God. Through that closeness, they figured many things out in ways that seem impossible to us. How many ancient cultures, like the Mayan and ancient Chinese, left records of their sophisticated understanding of mathematics and astronomy, even though they had no telescopes or calculators?

But today we think we are so smart, even though we have almost killed our entire planet. We have computers and spacecraft and 300 channels on our cable television set. But we still can't get along with each other or answer the fundamental questions of life and death. Our collective failures and our loss of spiritual wisdom prove that if you want to understand the truth about the spiritual world and where we come from, you get nowhere using man's brain. You cannot touch that issue through human learning and technology.

So even though religions may have made many mistakes, don't throw away the old wisdom from the ancient prophets. They may have understood more than we do about the truth of our being. However, realize that as an artificial human system, religion is also prone to being taken over by wrong interpretations and wrong thinking as it is passed down through many human hands. Its wisdom can point you in the right direction, but it cannot substitute for your own direct connection to God.

We Are All Connected

Because everything everywhere is made up of the same one universal energy, everything is tightly connected together. This one energy forms a "net" or network that touches everything in existence. This one universal energy is an unbroken thread that weaves through everything, connecting every part to every other part.

Human beings are also tightly connected. We should not see ourselves as 6.7 billion separate entities, but rather see ourselves as 6.7 billion cells of one person or one body. We influence each other far more than we know. Our lack of understanding that we are connected to each other causes many problems.

For example, if there is plague, famine and war in Africa, I cannot sit in my prosperous northern country and say, "I am so glad I am safe up here and unaffected by those terrible events happening in Africa." Or, "I am so lucky not to be drowned by that tidal wave that just hit Asia today." We like to think we are separate from those tragedies, but this is an illusion.

If a person has a gangrenous and cancerous tumor eating away their knee, it would be foolish for the ear or eye to say "Gee, I'm glad I am way up here on the head and not down there by that horrible tumor!" The sickness in the knee affects the whole body, and will, if untreated, spread and eventually kill the body – including the eye and ear. Why? The body is one piece, connected together.

When we ignore the fact that everything in the universe is alive, and that we are connected to it, we are foolish. We suffer from such a limited perspective on so many things that it makes us blind and deaf to the truth about humankind.

A dog can smell and hear things that a human being cannot. Its sensory range can pick up sound frequencies our human ears are deaf to. Because we are deaf to the same sounds a dog can hear, does that mean those sounds do not exist? Of course not. They exist. We think this room where we sit and read is very quiet, but a dog might think it's very noisy.

Similarly, our limited human perception is the reason why we do not feel connected to all that is around us. We cannot sense that everything from matter to the far reaches of space is made up of living energy. We miss out on many things and remain ignorant of so much information because of these limitations of ours. We conveniently think we are separate from the universe and not affected by tragedy happening to others.

If some leaders in big governments or big corporations silently think to themselves: "Let's ignore all those poor people in Africa. Let them all die. Let them butcher each other. Let AIDS wipe them out." No! That is wrong thinking. We are all connected. Every human being is one human being. We are all copied —split — from one original idea in God's mind. Our numbers today are a result of the division and duplication of that one original "Adam." Like one cell split into two, then into four, then eight, then into 6.7 billion cells to make one body. Our human race is like that. We are all connected, but we are ignorant of that fact.

So when we ignore Africa or Haiti or any other troubled place, it really is as foolish as the ear looking down at the knee and seeing that huge tumor and thinking "Boy look at that ugly thing! I'm so glad I'm better than that."

Instead, we should look at the people of Earth as if we were all cells of the same body. Some cells are on the bottom of the foot, some are intestinal cells, some are liver cells, and there are also a lot of bacteria in your gut that you need in order to survive. All of these cells look different, act or smell differently, but they're all linked together. Which cells do you want to die? Which do you think are unimportant? Cells in the same body should work together, communicate with each other, live in harmony and love each other in order for the entire body to survive. How can a body survive if the cells are taxing one another, resenting each other, fighting, stealing each other's food, or poisoning each other?

Those who consider themselves elite and better than others are foolish. They think they are so smart, when they are really so ignorant. For a moment let's pretend those elite are smarter. Let's pretend they are like a little group of brain cells talking to each other. "We don't need that foot. Why do we need that foot? We can sit here behind our computer and rule the world from our chair. Let's cut off our foot." Using the same logic, they later figure out that they don't need their legs either. So they chop off their legs. Even without legs, these elite cells figure they have all they need to be happy and rule the world. Eventually, they decide that they really only need two fingers to type into their computers, so they can afford to get rid of their whole body. Soon they are just a head with two robot fingers typing. Later they decide they don't really need anything but themselves, and so they eventually become two brain cells firing back and forth to each other. This is how silly "elitist" thinking is.

What is the truth? If one cell or a small group of cells in our body runs wild, takes all the nourishment for itself, inflates and starts crowding out other cells and killing them in the process, it's called "cancer." When they spread all over and try to kill everything, it's called "metastasis."

Unfortunately, our world's cancer of elitism, wrong thinking, corrupt systems and evil influence is metastasizing all over the world now through high technology, communication and transportation. Our advances are accelerating the speed of our own destruction.

We have even elevated our technologies over nature, thinking we are above it, that we aren't connected to nature, that we can be separate from and improve it. We forgot that Tao follows the natural way.

> *"Man following the earth,*
> *The earth follows heaven,*
> *And the heaven following the Tao,*
> *And the Tao following the Law of Nature."*
> Lao Tzu, *Tao Te Ching*, Chapter 25

But instead of following nature, we twist, use and ultimately damage nature. If Tao follows nature but we don't, how can we expect to follow Tao? We are left behind.

Tao's energy is so elusive, so much like nothingness, it's difficult for us to comprehend that it's everywhere. Be careful, because everywhere also means within bacteria, bees and ants. They have an intelligent internal program. That "nothingness" is what teaches them what to do. Don't tell me viruses and insects and bacteria are stupid. They have some very innovative and powerful ways to survive. See those insects that can change their form into leaves? Change colors to blend in? Look like sticks? They are a very low level of life form compared to human beings, but they, too, carry that original life energy.

If you cannot see that we are all connected, and you abandon nature and the natural way, and instead bet everything on man's artificial systems of science, knowledge, business and politics, not only will you fail to reach God, fail to reach Tao's frequency, you will have a total collapse sooner or later.

God is a Force of Balance

Students ask me "Why does Tao allow evil thinking to take over and lead the whole world to its destruction?" But I explain that the question they ask comes from a classic misunderstanding in western religion. They are still looking at God like a father figure, who judges morals and gets involved with every small detail of their lives.

It's not quite like that. It's not that Tao reaches down to deliberately hurt people or that it withholds any goodness back. God is constantly broadcasting a signal of balance, healing, mercy, nourishing and help. The trouble is that we cannot hear it. We can't or won't tune into that frequency.

Only people can hurt themselves. Our "sin" makes it so that we cannot see, cannot hear, cannot taste, and cannot feel truth. If you calm down and get rid of your sin – the artificial pollution, karma and bad energy that separates you from God's signal — suddenly you can hear, taste, see and know the right way to proceed to restore harmony and balance to your life.

The original energy of God is nothing like what we imagine, and it doesn't always necessarily match up with our rules of fairness or our expectations of what mercy is. We think God watches, gets involved in our personal affairs and controls this or that based on what we like or don't like. Then we get angry at God, or disbelieve in God, because God doesn't act according to our expectations and our little rules.

If we erase our misconceptions about how God does or doesn't act in our world, we can begin to see the truth. The energy of Tao is perfectly balanced and constantly at work trying to balance everything in the universe. When God works for balance and harmony, it takes into account *all* life, all beings, all dimensions, all of time, and all of creation.

How God works is more like this: If our world is tilted very far to one side, then it will need to tilt very far to the opposite side in order to be balanced again.

If we are so evil, so selfish and ruin so much, it's as if we have tilted our world very far to one side. We can look at our world and see that we are definitely far out of balance. In order to find balance, our world will have to swing very far in the opposite direction. God is the force that comes in to create that counterbalance action, to swing that pendulum back as far as it needs to go to counter the imbalance.

The trouble is that in this balancing act, we cannot survive either two extremes. We can't survive the extreme imbalanced world we are creating, nor can we survive the counterforce of God that will be necessary to correct our imbalance.

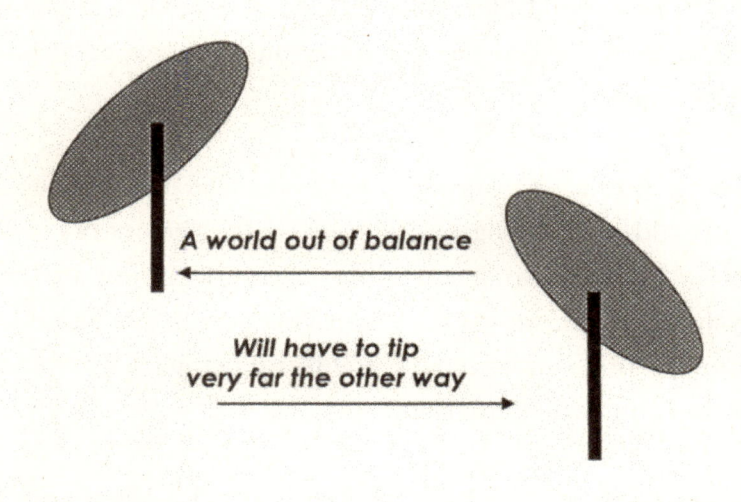

A world out of balance

Will have to tip very far the other way

If a critical mass of people tip our world to make it very unbalanced toward evil, it can pull the whole thing down. We may not survive when God wakes up and in accord with its nature of supreme balance, brings in the heavy counterforce and intervention necessary to rebalance this planet.

Natural disasters are not uncommon in our history, and neither are social upheavals and cosmic cataclysms. But do we really want to take things so far that this is what is required to set us back into balance again?

I'm here presenting this teaching in order to say: "Let's make the wobble less — not so extreme." Stop leaning so far away from nature, so disconnected from other people, so selfish and overreaching, so reliant on artificial systems and cutting ourselves off from the way of God. Let's reconnect and let God start to balance us sooner rather than later. It's not a matter of what's right or wrong. We are just off-balance.

Watching our world today is like watching a drunk driver weaving in and out of his lane. He says, "I'm doing okay." But you know that sooner or later he's going to crash. Worse than that, you are sitting in the car! You tell him to stop and let somebody else drive. But he brought booze and is passing it around the car, so everybody in the car is drunk. They all think his driving is just fine too. Can you imagine being the only sober person in that car?

Remember we likened this created universe to a dream of God. Everything that's happening everywhere is like a vast "Grand Dream" in the mind of God. But God can have a nightmare! We can become like a nightmare to that energy of God. Just like when we have a nightmare, it startles and wakes us up in order to shake that nightmare off. We can become so frightening and so off-balance that God will shake and startle in order to put an end to such a horrible dream. But God's thinking activity and power is so overwhelming, you don't want God to "wake-up."

If humans all had a baby's thinking, remained like Adam, so pure and so original, then it would be okay to wake up God. But look at our world! We are a nightmare! If we continue our descent, there will certainly be events that we feel are punishment, but it will not be based on moral issues. It will be because our activity became so horrifying and loud that we woke up that balancing force of God. That energy will immediately use its force of balance and power of instant materialization to correct this nightmare. Once again, it is not God punishing right and wrong. It is just balancing our imbalance. We are responsible. We caused the imbalance through our sin, and God's nature is to restore nourishing, mercy and balance.

It does not take a PhD to see how our planet cannot keep going the way it is with an increasing population of over 6.7 billion people. We try to solve the problem of feeding and providing for our massive world population by technology. We increase agriculture, increase fishing, and genetically modify everything. But the truth is that you can only push nature so far. Every natural process is its own balanced system.

For example, a lake is a system. You can dump a certain amount of junk into a lake each year, and because of its mechanism of tides, silt, and microscopic life, that lake can not only take in that junk and survive, but it will purify both that junk and itself. But if you keep dumping more and more junk into that lake, eventually, it's going to damage that delicate mechanism and the lake will die. Then it can no longer clean itself. It can't even support life. When that happens, it can take centuries, even eons, for nature to restore the natural mechanism, that system of balance, in that lake again.

Recently the Pope visited Australia, and in his talk he said he wants this world to focus on "thrift," and not to use up too many resources. But we've already gone over the breaking point for so many natural mechanisms, and our population still keeps growing.

A good analogy of our human situation is to pretend our earth is like a wonderful salad bar. God designed this salad bar to feed and supply everyone with enough to fill everyone's plate with what they need. If everyone took just a little of everything, just what they needed, the salad bar can perk along and replenish itself forever. This ever-replenishing and ever-renewing salad bar is so easy to manage, even a kid could do it.

So God gives it to a bunch of kids — meaning us — to manage. But one kid is rotten and he comes in and takes armfuls of food, eats more than his share, throws food on the floor and spits all over the other food, even takes off his shoes and walks all over the salad bar with his dirty feet. This kid disrupts the whole balance of the salad bar, because now there is not enough food, and not enough variety for everybody to get what they need. The salad bar can no longer function the way it was designed to work.

But instead of keeping this rotten kid in line, the other kids cower in the corner and say: "That's okay, you go ahead, there's enough here we can still manage to eat." They let the other kid continue to act like a spoiled brat.

Pretty soon lawyers come in and say "If you are going to sneeze you must turn 45 degrees away from the salad bar. There should be no shoes on the salad bar, but new shoes are okay." A businessman comes in and takes bags of food away from the salad bar and hides them. Later, when the salad bar is empty, he brings the food out to sell at a profit. The whole beautiful system becomes utter chaos, and some kids even start to starve.

At some point, God, who created this salad bar, will come and see what's going on and say: "Okay kids, that's enough playing salad bar – everybody out."

Is God cruel? If you had an aquarium and filled it with different species of fish, but you noticed that a few fish started attacking and eating the other fish, you might let it go on a little while. You might observe to see what was happening and whether it would stop on its own. But if the fish kept eating each other, at some point you'd take them all out, empty the aquarium, sort the fish into different tanks and start over.

Severe imbalance can lead to this whole system crashing down. The thing is, can enough of mankind cope with and survive such a drastic rebalancing event? Sure the earth will eventually return back to what it was, but it will take a long time. In the meantime, life may have to start over on this planet, evolving from bacteria up to a bug, etc...

When a tidal wave is coming, animals all run fast to higher ground long before it hits. They can feel it coming. Animals can also sense when an earthquake is about to happen. We can no longer feel those warning signals because our mind is clogged with signals of greed, lies and garbage. If you have a bad signal blaring inside you, not only can you not hear God's signal, not only do you not have that instinct, you will also be prone to listen to bad advice. "Hey, John! Look at how far the water pulled back! Let's go down to the beach and collect seashells to sell back home." "Okay!"

Just being honest helps so much. Keeping your mind clean and pure, and being able to hear and sense the signal from that original life energy will let you hear the right message about what you should do. But if you have lots of "knowledge," you'll have four or five smart ideas running around in your head and inevitably you will pick the wrong one at the worst possible time.

It's Easy to Worship the Wrong God
The real message is don't give your power to the devil: give your power to God only.

What is the dark force or devil? It is when you stay away from God so far or for so long that the original program of balance and harmony is distorted. The devil is God's power going to the wrong direction or straying from its original program by doing "too much" or "too little." When you enjoy or persist in staying away from that original program, or seek to travel further away, you give your power to that dark force. You worship the wrong god.

How do we worship the wrong god? One way is by creating artificial solutions to our problem and then looking for them to save us. We keep looking outside, to other things, other people, other ideas to solve our problems. We never consider turning inside and looking for God. Why do smartness, bad actions, personal agendas, and selfish calculation hurt us? They hurt us because as we accumulate more of these things, we stay further away from God. We create a cocoon of false knowledge around ourselves. That cocoon seals us off from connecting with God.

The true message is that you want to go back to your spiritual self. You can only "spiritualize" if you connect to God. That's why the world is so screwed up! We give our power to many things and many people other than God. The answer is to work inward to your own soul, to bring the volume of that correct signal up loud enough so that you can "hear" it again.

People abandon God and put their faith in false gods all the time. If I have a problem and contact the President of the United States because I think the President can help me, or if I go to a banker for my money problem, or if I trust that health insurance will protect me when I'm sick, I'm looking in the wrong direction for answers.

We strive for the goals we think will save us and improve our lives: luxury, money, profit, career, success or fame. There is nothing wrong with these things in themselves. It's people who went wrong. People manipulate things like luxury and money and fame. They make flashy things acquire status and deem them "very special." It is really a very childish way of thinking. Pretty soon everyone sees status items and accomplishments as very important. We seek them, take pride in them, and put them before God. Any time you place value in anything other than God, you start heading down the wrong track. That's the danger. Once again, we are lured into worshipping the wrong God.

Everything in this world like hospitals, our legal system, our educational system, our moral issues, what we consider as desirable or successful, are all man-made. Even if they are made out of good intention and love, evil thinking likes to grab hold of these systems particularly because so many people worship them. We have to work very hard and keep reminding ourselves over and over not to worship the wrong God.

In China, they worship ancestors. If you worship ancestors, you block God. Dictators like you to worship your father and grandfather, because then they can manipulate you. They'll print posters of themselves posed like a father holding a baby and you will subconsciously follow them, because that's how you're trained.

Doctors perform "miracles" and then they get worshipped like a false god. If I'm a doctor and I fix somebody, I should stay very humble. But they take credit and try to convince you that you need health insurance or more procedures so that they can stay in business and make more profit. Instead, they should take no credit, charge a fair price while they help others and give any healing credit to God.

Anybody blocking faith in God is evil. Anybody teaching you to worship something else, or blocking you from worshipping the real God is evil.

The worst thing we can do is insult our spiritual integrity — our Te. We do that by elevating our human dignity and human desires above our spiritual self. When we do that, we worship the wrong god. "Well I shouldn't invest in that company because it feels wrong inside, but everybody else is doing it and making a profit. If I don't, I'll fall behind or get left out, so I better join in quick." Such thinking insults your spiritual soul. When you do that, you worship the wrong god and tune into the wrong frequency. You will experience suffering one way or another when you choose the wrong god.

When I tell people that they worship the wrong god, they wonder, "Are you criticizing me?" I'm not at all. Everybody worships the wrong god. Nobody is immune. At any moment, you can worship the wrong god without knowing it.

The journey back to the original God is a constant journey, one that requires ongoing attention. Let's explore the tools we need to make that journey back to the real God.

PART FOUR: Restoring Our Connection to God

道

Moving Meditation is Our Main Tool

God and human being — we try to link. Every moment of every day, God is reaching toward us wanting to connect. But we don't know how to reach back in return.

We try to understand the way God works with our mind. But because we are human beings, our mind is trapped in this limited dimension, so we cannot. Since we cannot understand it in our current condition, only changing ourselves can enable us to sense, understand and connect back to God.

If you try to reach God by reading about God, thinking about God, talking about God, having a party about God, joining a social activity or association devoted to God, this is a trap. Those activities don't make the necessary fundamental change in you. Your only way back to God is to learn how to correctly reprogram and actually change yourself.

We need to learn how to make that change and restore that original ability to contact God. We have that latent original ability inside us because we have life energy and we also have Te. Those two tools are what we need. But first we need to be able to feel our life energy, strengthen and purify it, and then use that life energy to feel and connect to our Te.

The main tool we use to relearn how to feel life energy is *moving meditation*. Moving meditation can also help us strengthen and purify our life energy in order to raise our energy frequency. Only when your life energy is pure and strong can you feel and penetrate that Te inside you.

Moving meditation means meditate and move. But not only that, it also means to feel and move your life energy. If you just meditate, you will be stuck in your mind and have a hard time feeling and using that life energy. If you only move, you will be merely doing physical exercise. You must combine both movement and meditation in order to really feel and work with your life energy.

There are many systems surviving today that can teach you how to meditate, but there is only one system that preserves the true teaching of moving meditation as a way to raise your energy and reconnect to God. That system is the true and ancient teaching of Taichi accompanied by Tao Gong meditation (Tao Gong means "Tao's work" — the work to transform ourselves in order to reach Tao.)

Real Taichi training can be very hard to find. The Taichi we are talking about here is not merely slow motion exercise. It is a system of deep and powerful moving meditation that can bring up that true feeling of life energy, or "Chi," and teach you how to strengthen and use that energy.

We are Like Cell Phones
Your cell phone is a piece of equipment that is capable of many amazing things. You can call somebody next door or on another

continent. Other people can call your cell phone and instantly talk to you no matter where you are.

However, unless your cell phone can power up and connect to that cellular energy network in the sky — the broadcast band between towers and satellites that carries messages from one phone to another — your cell phone is worthless. You might as well use it as a paperweight, or use it to pound nails into a board.

Each human being is like a cell phone. Our life energy inside gives us the capacity to connect to and communicate with that "network" of Tao energy that connects all things. Yet the vast majority of people today are like broken cell phones. Human beings living in this limited dimension are damaged and have lost their original abilities. They can no longer power up and connect back to that network — to that one universal energy.

To take advantage of its high technology, you also need to know what a cell phone is for and how to use one; otherwise it is useless to you. Imagine a caveman finding a cell phone somebody left on the beach. Without knowing how to turn it on or what it's for, a caveman might use it to crack oysters or throw it as a weapon against somebody.

Because we have Chi and we have Te, we have a tremendous innate capacity to be far more than we are, but most of us don't know it. Just like that caveman, our cell phone is worth nothing unless we know *how* to use it and actually connect to that network of universal energy, the Tao.

The reason our connection to the Tao is so broken and hard to re-establish, is that our Te, that piece of God inside of us, is insulated with very slow material. We are layered with insulation from this physical and artificial world. Even with Taichi training, it can be hard for our energy to pierce through the many layers of heavy, slow, and even negative energy to reach our Te and get on that network.

That's why we must practice and keep refining ourselves through moving meditation. Moving meditation will allow us to pierce through that insulation to repair our "cell phone." Repair means I upgrade myself, purify myself, return to my original way of listening, feeling, and seeing. I can connect to my Te and pick up any signal in the entire universe. I can gain all knowledge and information anywhere, past or future, from that universal energy network. I can do that if I successfully repair my "cell phone."

Repairing that cell phone is critical. When we can use our life energy and contact that Te, we begin to see the truth about how we are connected to the world around us. Expanding our perception, we live more effectively. We can gain critical information about our lives and the world around us. We can make use of the laws of the universe, rather than blindly violating those laws and causing suffering for ourselves and others. We can perceive the higher energies of the spiritual dimension, and choose to work with them or avoid them.

What's more, we can use that connection to communicate back and forth with the one universal energy that is the source of our being – that intelligent one universal power called "Creator," "God," "Source," or "Tao."

Our priority, our urgent task in this life, is to reconnect to our Source. We know we have the capacity to reconnect, so where do we begin? Since we are damaged and need repair, we have to fix our cell phone.

But to fix a cell phone is a sophisticated process. We cannot use a hammer or the wrong cleaning fluids. The wrong method will further damage our cell phone's ability to function. We need the right tools to repair our cell phones, and the right instructions to restore our connection to the universal energy network. We have to find the precise way to reprogram ourselves so that we can bring back our power to both listen and talk to God.

We Must Learn How to Return to God

Spiritual and religious teachings abound all over the world. There are also countless so-called experts or teachers who claim to know about the life energy or Chi. This can make it very difficult to find the real information that will show us how to restore our life energy and our connection to God. Imagine that you are looking for a real twenty-dollar bill in a sea of counterfeit twenty-dollar bills, how would you even find it?

You can spend your entire life reading dozens of books, attending sermons and lectures and seminars, and devote years of your life and thousands of dollars to every teaching that comes along, and still get nowhere. Sure you will be entertained, and may even learn some fascinating theories and beliefs. Maybe you will even see miracles and wonders of a spiritual origin. Yet in the end, if you have not been able to restore your life energy to the strength and purity necessary to reconnect back to that one true God, where will it leave you?

At the same time, it is very hard to reach God without help. It is hard to understand *"how to"* and raise your energy without a master, without a tried and true method that others have used to successfully reach the same goal. It is imperative to find the real teaching that shows you *"how to."*

The fact that you may now even slightly glimpse the urgency of restoring your life energy (so that you can reach Te in order to reconnect with God) puts you many steps ahead on this journey. To know what you yet need to learn means you are blessed. Why? Because now you can start real work on your energy and make real progress. Once you start to work in the right way, the real transformation can begin.

Moving meditation is the primary tool you will use. However, in order to do moving meditation the right way, we have to adjust our lifestyle, learn the right way of thinking and fully understand the situation we are in if we are going to get out of that situation. We have to think right so that we can slowly build a lifestyle and frame of mind that supports our moving meditation.

Within the wisdom of this ancient teaching, there is a process of how to qualify ourselves. We have to take time to work on this process step by step. Let's review our goal again, and then explore more tools and ways of thinking that will help us reach that goal.

The Real Goal of Taichi

While it may seem odd to those who have never experienced it, the first step to connect back to the network of Tao is Taichi. You may scratch your head and ask, "How can that slow dance they do in the park, that strange Chinese martial art, repair my connection to God?"

Actually, what most people don't know, even long time Taichi students, is that the ultimate task of mending our connection to God is the real goal of ancient Taichi and always has been. This is because moving meditation in sincere and correct Taichi practice can replenish and raise the frequency of our life energy.

The sad thing is that most Taichi taught today has completely lost sight of that goal. Taichi is taught today mostly as nothing more than "slow-motion exercise." People do not experience the profound changes Taichi can offer, because they often learn from well-meaning instructors who never understood its ancient purpose. It is neither the student nor the instructor's fault. The real purpose and training of this art has been veiled for centuries, even from Chinese practitioners.

In my first book, *T'ai Chi Classics*, I describe how Taichi evolved in the ancient Tao temples but was stolen by martial artists to help them augment their fighting skills. We are lucky that Taichi was stolen by the martial artists because they were the ones to preserve the art when the temples were destroyed through the many political upheavals in China's history. But because of them, Taichi has been passed down in a teaching style suited to martial arts more than to Taichi's original purpose. As a result, over the years that original purpose and the core power of the original temple teachings have almost been lost.

In addition, Taichi's popularity exploded and continues to explode in a very public way across the western world. However, in its breakneck speed of growth, few people stopped to question the real purpose behind these slow and strange movements. Many Taichi students enjoy it simply as a relaxing form of exercise that yields health benefits. True, it is enjoyable and beneficial, but it can be so much more.

Real Taichi that is taught and practiced the right way will transform you so much that over time you will feel like a completely different person. Taichi, when practiced the right way under the guidance of a master, will profoundly change your internal nature. If you practice Taichi for a long time and settle only for mastering a few martial arts moves, or feel satisfied with a few minor health benefits, you join the millions who have missed Taichi's highest goal.

We are not simply trying to improve ourselves. Our goal is complete and total change. If you are satisfied with a little improvement in yourself and then go no further, you will miss the true purpose of Taichi. What's our purpose? We are aiming for total self-transformation!

Once you, through Taichi, can connect to the center of your life energy, your Te, you will be forever changed. If you are Mary, you will no longer feel like Mary. If you are Bob, you will no longer feel like Bob. Be careful not to accept improvement short of the true goal. Have you been totally and completely transformed?

An analogy I like to use for this transformation is the change that would happen if a rabbit transformed completely and turned into a cat. If I am a rabbit, I like to eat grass and hop around. I get scared when other animals look at me. I have long ears, a stubby tail, and nice soft fur.

Now I can practice some martial arts or weight lifting and become a bigger, faster and stronger rabbit, or eat more carrots and become a sleeker, healthier rabbit. However, even though I've worked on myself and see many nice changes, I am still a rabbit.

What we are talking about is to use Taichi to completely transform your nature. First you are a rabbit, and then one day you feel totally different. You have completely transformed to become a cat! You have no interest in eating grass. Other animals no longer scare you. Instead of you running away from them, they run away from you! You move, feel, look and sound totally different than before. Your total nature has changed. You are still you, but you are totally transformed.

This Taichi teaching is not meant to merely improve you. We are not making you into a stronger, better rabbit. Make no mistake.

This Taichi teaching, the real Taichi training, is designed to totally change your nature.

We are not interested in a *"quantity"* change — making you calmer, kinder, a little bit healthier, or better able to perform 200 new Taichi forms that you didn't know last year. We are interested in a *"quality"* change. With a quality change, you are a whole new person!

Actually this whole new person is no stranger. This is the real You! The You that has been hidden under layers of time, pollution and wrong thinking. The You that was forgotten as you grew up, left to the side, ignored and buried. The You that enjoys a natural and spontaneous connection to the original energy of the Universe! That old rabbit you is gone.

How does Taichi change your fundamental nature? Taichi can teach you how to focus your mind like a laser beam, burning through all of the pollution and distractions of the artificial world. Taichi can help you raise your energy frequency so high that negative energy and attachments simply fall away because they can no longer cling to you. Taichi can help you peel away the insulation coating your Te so that your cell phone can reach the network of Tao. Taichi is the tool to bring back your connection to God. This is the real goal and experience of Taichi mastery.

Taichi heals the separation between you and the One living energy of the universe. Every round of moving meditation purifies and strengthens your Chi. The purer your Chi, the better your chance of connecting with the piece of original energy inside you — the Te that connects you back to that network of Tao.

Without moving meditation that transformation is impossible. Without it, we cannot develop our life energy, Chi. We can't tell our life energy what we want it to do or where to go because we can't communicate with it. Our Chi does not listen to us because it cannot hear us. Our mind is too rough and coarse to penetrate the Chi. It's as if we are speaking the wrong language. Taichi is like learning the right language that our Chi can respond to.

The right language, the language of Chi, is found in the pure dedicated feeling you build through moving meditation. That is why we practice, so as to be able to learn to use pure feeling. This is what the Chi can understand. This is what the Chi will respond to. Then we can communicate with our Chi, tell it what we need and where we want it to go. We can strengthen that Chi and make it pure. Then it can reach our Te — that piece of original energy inside us that is connected to Tao.

Taichi is Like a Refining Oven
Many old Taoist texts refer to "internal alchemy" or refining yourself like steel. Alchemy is the process by which ordinary metal is turned into gold. We refine steel by burning off impurities and changing its very nature. In Taichi, that is exactly what we are trying to do. We are trying to burn off our impurities and contamination and refine ourselves to so great an extent, that our very nature changes.

In the old allegories, Taoist alchemy takes place in an oven. It may be Lao Tzu's oven, a "Bagua" oven or an eight-sided oven. What do these allegories mean? What is this oven and how are we refined inside of it? All those old Taoist writings are very hard to understand because they were written in code. If you did not have access to a master's teaching to reveal the hidden meaning, the writings would seem strange and incomprehensible.

The oven is the place in which our transformation occurs – that place is our practice. The fire and heat inside the oven is the powerful force of meditation – specifically, moving meditation. The eight sides of that alchemical oven are the eight directions we move in our moving meditation – forward, backward, right, left, up, down, inward and outward.

When we learn correct Taichi form, meaning correct physical movement, correct breathing, correct relaxation, correct energy flow and execution of the form, it is as if we are building the physical structure of an oven. We are laying the brick walls, brick floor and a fireproof ceiling. We build a solid door. We construct a seamless seal to keep all the heat inside. The better we build our oven, the more heat it can retain and the better it will cook what we put inside.

That's why proper Taichi practice and instruction is so critical. You need to learn the correct way to perform Taichi. You need to learn the principles of how energy flows so that you know what makes one form correct and another less effective. You need to know how to flow your energy in all eight directions. You need to practice enough and strive for perfection so that eventually your physical form is balanced, correctly aligned, relaxed, and full, round and smooth. The better your instructor, the better corrections you will receive in order to reach a higher quality of practice. The better your form and the better your practice, the better you will be able to build your oven.

But you can't spend your whole life just building an oven. Some people spend decades just perfecting their physical Taichi form. Others spend decades collecting many different styles of forms: Yang style, Chen style, Wu style, government style, etc. They spend all their time merely acquiring a "quantity" change: increasing the quantity of forms they know, or clocking a quantity of hours in physical practice.

We do not want to make that mistake. We are working for a "quality" change, not just a "quantity" change. We can't spend decades merely laying the brick to build an oven. We want to cook something! An oven is useless until we add fire! That fire is the power of our focused, calm meditative mind. When we add the high frequency power of mind to our Taichi form through moving meditation, we are adding fire to our oven. Then we can cook something! We can make a "quality change."

You can't cook anything with a brick oven if you don't have any fire. But likewise, you can't cook very well if you have fire but your oven is flimsy or not built right. That won't work either. The heat will escape, the fire will go out, or your oven will burn up. That's why sitting meditation alone, or moving meditation with an imbalanced or sloppy physical Taichi form, will also prevent you from making the quality change you are looking for.

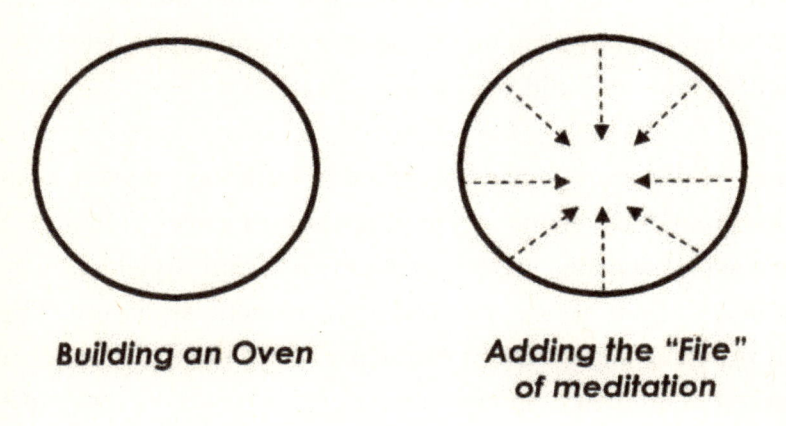

Building an Oven

Adding the "Fire" of meditation

But when you have both a good fire and a good oven — moving meditation done with correct Taichi form — then you have a very hot oven. Now you can cook something! Now you can transform! The more concentrated and focused your meditation, with less distraction and mind wandering, the hotter your fire.

To transform yourself, you need to subject yourself to that oven. You need to put yourself in there as often and for as long as possible in order to burn off impurity and change yourself. If you only stick one hand in there, it won't work. If you only jump in the oven for three seconds, that's not long enough. If your fire is only 90 degrees, that's not hot enough. You need enough time in the oven and enough intense "heat" to cause a total transformation.

The Goal of our Transformation

What's our goal in subjecting ourselves to this transforming oven called moving meditation? No less than reconnecting with God.

To be able to communicate with our Creator, our Source, our "God" or Tao, is the true goal of what some call "prayer." Prayer is the ability to successfully connect to the one ultimate God, as well as the ability to both transmit and receive a clear message to and from God.

For centuries, religious and spiritual people have wondered, "Why do prayers sometimes work and sometimes not?" There are two primary issues that define whether you can truly pray and reach that one true God or not. The first is, "Can you transmit?" The second is, "How clear is the content of your transmission?"

To connect, receive and transmit requires that we be able to raise our own energy frequency. Our frequency has to be high and pure enough to match the frequency of that "Net."

We must also be able to send and receive our messages to and from the right place. That means we must be powerful and clean enough to pierce through all of those layers in the spiritual dimension to reach the one true God, not landing short.

Imagine if we are trying to call God, but instead only reach the shopping channel or the local pizza parlor. That means our cell phone is not yet fully functional. If your message broadcasts just high enough to reach one of those small "gods," or worse, one of the spiritual beings traveling away from God, they may hear and pick-up your call. You might actually receive an answer to your prayer. But will it be an answer you want? Will that "answer to prayer" deceive you into thinking you have reached the real God?

Let's say we can connect to the one real and true God, we still have to be able to send and receive a clear and true message. A cell phone that can only send a garbled message, or receives calls that are muffled by static interference, is still a broken cell phone. We want to say "I love you God." Instead, that message goes out as "*Blub, garg, babble, gabble.*" Or worse, God wants to communicate to us, but all we hear is static. So we must clean our cell phone so that its transmission is crystal clear.

All of these tricky obstacles are why priests and religious seekers wonder: "Why do prayers sometimes work and most times not?" "I want to reach God but how can I do that?" "Is the voice I hear inside from Tao or something else?" These are questions of connection. The trial and error of prayer through the years is a record of success and failure in that effort to connect.

It is our job, our duty in this lifetime, to do whatever we can to repair our "cell phone." We must urgently re-establish our connection to our ultimate Source, to join back to the mainframe network so that we may be in balance with the harmony of the universe. We must also clean up our energy so that we can both broadcast and receive clear and true messages. But how do we know when and if we are headed in the right direction? How do we know if we pray to the right place?

If you carry around a coating of negative energy, you will automatically pull in a signal that matches the frequency of that negative junk. It will be impossible to find the clean and pure signal of Tao.

So-called negative energy can be wrong thinking, the consequences of past or present negative actions (karma or "sin"), pollution we pick up from our environment (mental, spiritual and physical toxins we are exposed to during our day), or anything else that prevents us from resonating with the pure and original signal of Tao. It is this negative energy coating inside us that is like insulation, preventing our cell phone from connecting to that mainframe.

That is why we use Taichi. In Taichi practice we work to make our energy both strong and pure. You need to be strong in order to break through that interference. But you need to be pure in order to make the right connection. Many Taichi practitioners reach a state of very strong Chi, but if it is not pure, it cannot connect back to the ultimate true God. Others are able to refine their Chi to be very clean and pure, but if it is not strong, it will fail to pierce through the barriers of insulation and reach that connection.

That's why true connection to Tao requires both strength and the utmost purity. To develop strong Chi is a matter of correct practice in Chi flow in your moving meditation — flowing your energy, not just moving your body. To develop pure and clean Chi, on the other hand, we must strive for pure sincerity.

Once we feel our sincerity is pure, we keep working to exchange that sincerity for an even purer sincerity, and then an even purer sincerity, and on and on. Why? When we reach the ability to connect to those higher frequencies of energy, utmost sincerity is important so that we are not fooled into connecting with the wrong "god," landing short of our ultimate goal.

That is why a sense of humility is vital in our work toward sincerity. We are never satisfied, but humbly continue, with no discount, to insist on even greater purity and sincerity within ourselves. We continuously work to clean our minds, our lives and our energy from the negativity that can so easily creep back in and cling to us. And the higher we go, the higher our vigilance. During this process, we continue flowing our energy, practicing and practicing so that our energy becomes stronger as we refine ourselves.

Before acquiring this high degree of strength and purity, our energy was like a light bulb. We may have shone, but our energy was weakly spread and diffused all over. After such training, we can harness our energy like a laser beam — focused and pure — and aim it exactly where we want to go.

Where we want to go is back to our Te, that piece of God inside us. Why? That pure Te knows how to transmit to and from the true ultimate God with no wrong numbers and no static interference. That Te has a tunnel or "wormhole" directly through all of that insulation and straight back to Tao. That is why Te is the secret to making a direct connection.

Establishing Your Lifestyle

Reconnecting with Tao through our Te is simply a flip of the mind back to the purest state of sincerity. But what is pure sincerity, and how can we reach that state?

We have years of wrong thinking, layers of accumulated artificial notions and negative energy that prevent us from being truly sincere. These are the same layers of heavy insulation that we must scrape away or burn through in order to connect to Tao.

First of all, we must see the artificial world for what it is, and stop making it our goal. You cannot beam a straight and steady signal to God if that signal is pulled off target by the lure of other priorities. The Bible speaks of this when it says that no man can serve two masters at the same time. It even gives an example: "You cannot serve both God and money." What it is trying to tell you is that any time your focus is divided, you cannot be sincere. To reach the frequency of God, you can have no other goal but God.

Is money evil? Of course not. There is nothing wrong with money and luxury and the comfort they provide. But to be useful, they need to be seen in their proper and most productive role. A proper role for money is for it to serve us by allowing us the leisure and the ability to cultivate ourselves and practice. That is money and luxury's best and rightful role in our lives. Seeing money this way is how prosperity can become a lasting blessing instead of a distracting curse. Money can be used to keep God as a priority in your life and help you strengthen your frequency in that direction.

Instead, for most people, money becomes like an anchor pulling them down and away from God. Luxury and comfort become a distraction or even a hindrance to their spiritual goal. Why? Earning, managing, investing, and accounting for one's money and possessions can burn up much personal energy and time. It can also bring frustration, stress, and anxiety, or social and family pressures. More money often brings more complication into one's life rather than less.

You need a lot of self-discipline and wisdom to manage money in a way that reduces rather than increases complication and stress in your life. Few people are able to do it. Remember, it's all about your energy frequency. Can you manage your money in a way that it helps you raise your frequency rather than lower it?

There is another, more insidious way that money and luxury can lower our energy frequency. If my life is very rich and comfortable, I may enjoy myself so much that I never question what is going on around me. I live a protected and sheltered life and never get the deep sense that something is wrong with our human dimension. I'm never truly motivated wholeheartedly to seek other answers. I may even get the wrong idea that I am going in the right direction spiritually, because everything is so pleasant. I'm so comfortable that I never put forth the effort necessary to raise my internal energy. In this way, riches can again become the obstacle of sincerity. A few rich people are lucky enough to be like Buddha. Even though he was a prince, he yearned to see past the illusion of comfort and privilege to find the solution to birth, death, aging and illness.

This is why in many religious traditions suffering is seen as a blessing of sorts. This is not to say suffering is a virtue, but that at least when we suffer we realize something is not right. It can motivate us to seek a way out. We become willing to work hard at doing whatever is necessary to find God, to learn how to pray effectively and to become sincere.

Money is just one example we can use. Other matters in our life can also get in the way of our sincerity if we let them – our career, our family, or our social and leisure pursuits. There is nothing wrong with a comfortable and pleasant life. However if our work toward these other areas of life adds more stress than we can bear, or if these goals dominate and drain our energy, they can only hinder our ability to restore the sincerity we need to connect to our original energy.

Ideally, we should seek just enough comfort in our life to make it easier to spend time in meditation and practice. We need just enough prosperity in our lives to avoid undue hardship and strain. Our goal is finding that balance where our outer life contributes to rebuilding our life energy instead of depleting it.

This is one reason why I tell my students that a right "lifestyle" is one of the critical aspects of their practice. It can take quite a bit or work to maintain a balanced and stable lifestyle that leaves you the time, freedom and peace of mind for sincere practice. Maintaining such a lifestyle is its own form of practice and can be an ongoing challenge.

Every individual is different. What *you* need to feel and live in balance is different from what another person needs. Also, everyone has different destinies, different obligations and different recycled energy to reconcile in this life. Another person may need more resources to accomplish his destiny and fulfill his obligations.

Whatever your lot in life, whether you walk a hard or an easy road, use whatever you have to start your journey back to Tao. Let the outer matters of your life contribute to your sincerity, not detract from it. Let nothing come between you and your goal. Let nothing come between you and God.

Taichi Meditation and Sincerity

Developing true sincerity is why we work so hard at pure moving meditation in Taichi. Our students learn that "when I move forward, there is nothing but forward. And when I move backward, there is nothing but backward." This form of training fuses thinking, feeling, movement, body, breath and soul into one pure and sincere intention. Once you can do that, then you can move as one connected whole. This is part of the real practice and energy work of developing total sincerity. When every part of you is united and joined together and focused toward one point, there is no room for insincerity.

Our mind is like light. Like we said earlier, before Taichi training, our mind shines like a light bulb – diffuse and shining outward in all directions. Taichi training shows you how to condense and focus this light like a laser. When the time comes to connect back to the energy frequency of Tao, this trained, pure, calm and laser-like mind can easily penetrate through the many layers that separate us from Tao, and deliver a pure and clear message. Without such ability, there is virtually no way to do so.

The more Taichi you do, the more you will gradually loosen and scrape away those impurities inside you. You find yourself making better choices that are more in harmony with the original and natural way life is supposed to be. As you restore your connection to the feeling of your pure and original life energy, the attraction of artificial, negative and meaningless activities gradually lose their appeal. As your health improves, you make better choices about the foods you eat and how to maintain the environment around you for even better health. As your energy increases, old destructive behavior falls away.

This gradual transformation in turn naturally increases your sincerity in all things. This improvement feeds back into your Taichi, which becomes more focused and sincere and in turn brings even more benefits. With this positive feedback loop, Taichi becomes an ever-ascending, ever-rewarding journey.

The original program of harmony that beams from the original energy is constantly broadcasting out through the whole universe. It is ready to restore and heal and bring things back into their original balance. The trouble is that we cannot pick up this signal loud and clear enough for it to make a difference in our lives.

We can improve our ability to tune in and respond to this original program and signal through moving meditation. Even raising your energy a little bit can bring in that signal just a little bit louder. It is as if God is always calling and reaching for us. Right now we cannot hear that call or touch that hand, but as we learn to reach and call back with more and more sincerity, some day we can hope to bridge the gap.

This is a marvelous prospect. The trouble is that most human beings do not bother to try. Those that want to try have lost access to the training that shows them how to do it. Until now.

Our Common Sense Cannot Comprehend
Sincerity gives you the ability to concentrate with no distraction or blockages. Your mind becomes so pure, so original, that your frequency is right next to the frequency of life energy, which is in turn right next to the frequency of Tao. A mind at that high frequency pulls on the Net and that Net starts to move.

Moses opening up the Red Sea is an example of how true sincerity or "faith" can move that whole Net. Moses' sincerity reached all the way to God. He and his people were trapped with soldiers driving them into the sea. It was "do or die," with no time for distraction or blockage. Anytime someone touches that super-Net with real sincerity, it causes things to change.

This ultimate energy of the universe has always been and is always there. It was never created and will never disappear. This energy is like mind – a "super-mind." You cannot feel or understand it unless you are trained. Only when you raise yourself to a higher energy frequency will you then be better able to understand how the universe works.

Take spiritual travel, for example. The stories of old Taoist immortals say that they could pass through walls or travel from one city to another in the blink of an eye. How they did that seems like a mind-boggling mystery. But it's not mysterious when you understand how Tao works.

Let's say I want to travel from New York to San Francisco by digging a tunnel through the Earth. It may take me 5,000 years. If I decide to travel to San Francisco by walking across the surface of the earth, it might take only two years. If I go up a little bit higher and sit on top of a bicycle I can coast along on wheels and it might take me a couple weeks. If I go up further to a jet airplane's level, the trip from New York to San Francisco takes only 4 hours. Now, if I could launch a rocket ship from New York, it might land in San Francisco in about 30 minutes. The higher I go, the less resistance I meet and the quicker I can travel.

Take this analogy further and imagine I could go to an even higher level with zero resistance. All I would need to do is think "San Francisco" and I am there. That is what it's like when you connect to this super-highway of Tao. (There are stories about Taoists who practiced that sort of "travel" as recently as 1910. They would get together and make bets with each other over who could meditate and bring something back from very far away: like a flower from Florida.)

It's hard for us to understand that type of power. It's inconceivable to us. Our attempt to understand how the "super-highway" of God works is like a dog trying to understand how our human world works.

If you tell your dog, "Look, boy, we are going on an airplane and in maybe four hours or so, you'll see Grandma and play fetch with Suzy in California. We'll stay there for a week, and then fly back home. Okay, Fido?" He has no idea what you are trying to tell him. The dog will look at you, pant, wag his tail, and his eyebrows will screw up like he is trying to understand. But no matter how hard he tries, he cannot comprehend this. He cannot even fathom this idea.

So let's say you take Fido on that plane to California and then come back. Once you drive home from the airport, you let Fido out of the car. Fido runs out into the backyard to talk to Spike, the dog next door. He says, "*Bark,* you wouldn't believe it. *Woof,* we go up, come down, I'm in a totally different place. *Woof,* smells different, different people, *woof,* couple days later and we are up in the sky again and now I'm home, *pant... pant... pant....*"

Spike sniffs Fido's tail and says, "*Woof,* nonsense! You're crazy! That can't happen!" Spike starts to gossip. Pretty soon all the dogs in the neighborhood think Fido is crazy and they start to avoid him. But Fido was there! He still believes.

In a dog's world, a dog might be able to go to Grandma's house in California on his own power. It might take three years, but by using his smell and intuition, he might get himself there with a little luck. But when he went up in that airplane, Fido experienced another way of travel completely outside of a dog's world.

It sounds so mysterious and difficult to us. But actually, when you understand how God works, it's quite logical. After all, if God is one piece, what does travel mean to God? If I want to travel between where I'm sitting and my little finger, what do I do? The distance between me and my finger is right here! How do I travel instantly from here to California? I don't have to travel across space, I simply shrink space! I shrink space because I am space. When you are capable of reconnecting with that power it opens a whole range of possibilities that defy our logic.

Scientists and physicists talk about this, but they are still tied down. Some are afraid to pursue these matters. It's as if they think, "If I cannot convince the other dogs, then I am not a scientist."

In order for a dog to understand how he got to California and back, he would have to transform himself. He would have to raise his frequency of mind and life energy. How far do I have to move from being a dog to being a human? Not very far. In the relative range of life forms, a dog and human are very close. Likewise, we need to transform ourselves just enough to touch that superhighway network of God's energy. Those old masters let us know that this is possible. Because it is possible and not unreachable, we need to devote every bit of effort toward such a quality change.

Life Energy: Restoring the Power of the Single Cell

Your life energy is the most important treasure you possess. Without it, you have nothing. Even if you are a brilliant genius, or have billions of dollars in investments, or an enormous loving family and thousands of friends, or even if you are a famous world leader or movie star, without your life energy you are nothing.

Life energy is like the number "1" in the number 1,000,000. Without that "1" you are left with only zeroes. Everything else in your life is another zero attached to your "1." The more zeroes you have, the bigger or richer you think you are. But if you take away that "1," you really have nothing. What is your wealth without your life? What is your family to you if you die? What are all your interests and endeavors to you if you have no life energy?

Life energy should be our top priority. The problem is that we spend our whole life chasing more zeros, driving up the number of things we possess and experiences we enjoy. We never spend a single moment to appreciate and build up and protect that number "1" – our life energy.

It is time to reverse that. Change the focus of your attention away from the zeros that make your life seem so big, and spend time with your life energy. Spend time in moving meditation to make that life energy pure and strong. Protect that number "1".

Many people feel that time spent in meditation or Taichi or studying ancient wisdom is somehow less valuable than time making money or lifting weights or going on a great vacation.

This is because in the beginning, the results of your practice are hard to see. But as time goes on, you start to feel the changes.

Time spent learning about and developing your life energy is the most powerful time you can spend and the wisest investment you will ever make. You are tapping into the greatest power of all, the power of life!

Nobody understands the power of life. For example, nobody understands this one primary thing: What power makes that first cell split? What tells it to do that? What enables it to do that? Nobody can answer that.

What actually happens is a lesson in the power of Tao at work. The cell itself is formed when two forces join together — sperm and egg, Yin and Yang. Before that first single cell splits, it begins to pull itself inward before it bounces back outward and expands. It expands so much, that it splits itself into two. The two cells have just as much power to split again into four. And those four have the power to split again, and again, and again, to form an embryo.

Can you imagine the power it takes to split yourself into two? Can you do that right now? Can you stand there all by yourself and with all your adult intelligence and muscles, will yourself apart into two living people? The strongest person in the world could not do that.

But once upon a time, that's exactly what you did. At one time, you were capable of this. When? When you were that single cell! You had and still have such power! That tremendous intelligent and unimaginable power comes from the original dimension.

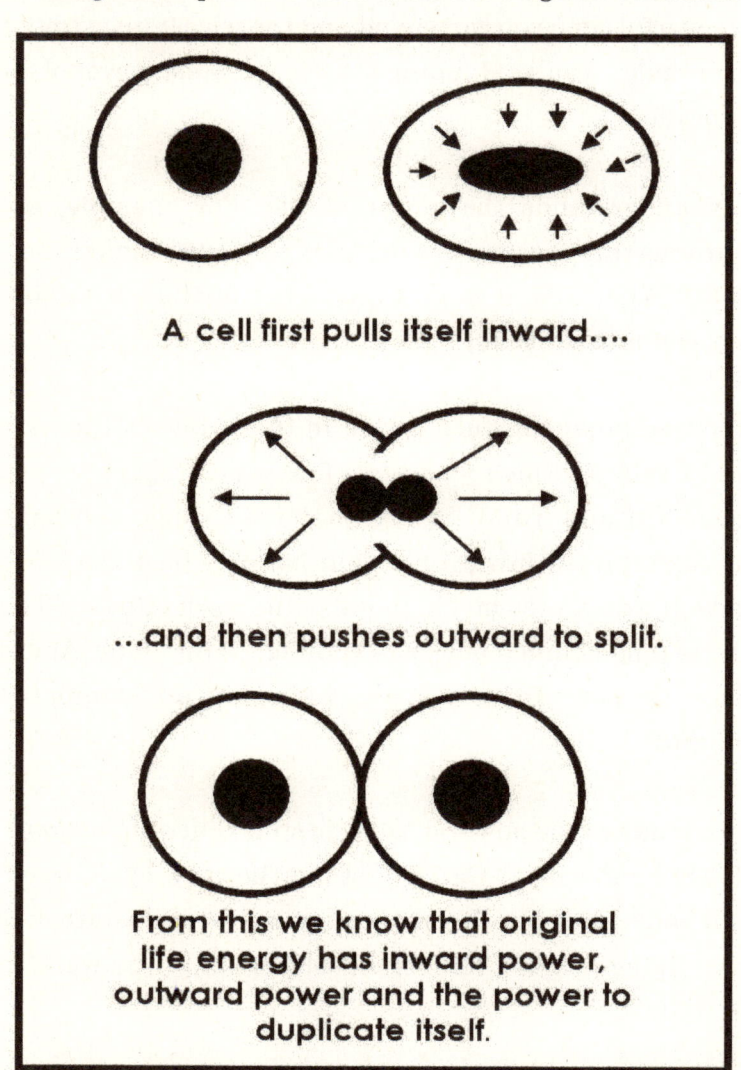

A cell first pulls itself inward....

...and then pushes outward to split.

From this we know that original life energy has inward power, outward power and the power to duplicate itself.

Did you know that before this moving meditation was given the name "Taichi" by Chang Sen Feng, it was called *"prenatal meditation?"* We do forms like *"Inward and Outward"* and *"Split."* We are trying to wake up that primary memory from before we were born, the memory of that power we still possess, the power of the first cell splitting itself into two living cells. We are looking for that memory so we can access that power.

We have that power inside of us, although we are unaware of it. That tremendous cell-division power is still going on millions of times a day in our bodies. If our cells didn't have that power, we'd die. If you cut yourself, that's how you heal. Those cells divide and make copies of themselves to repair your injury. Imagine what would happen if they could not.

Finding that true original signal can benefit our health. Did you know that aging is partly due to the cells' fading memory of proper cell division? That's why everything runs down when you age, that ability of cells to make copies of themselves wears down or gets warped. They can no longer duplicate themselves as perfectly or efficiently as before. Eventually that original energy is so weak and damaged it can no longer divide at all. When that happens, your major organs will start to deteriorate and you will ultimately die.

You are not supposed to die. Theoretically, if that cell division mechanism stays intact, strong and perfect, like when you were a newborn, you could go on indefinitely. Part of Taichi's health benefit is that by practicing real Taichi, we can remind our cells how they used to be and help restore their ability to respond to that original energy program of inward, outward, divide and split.

Our Body, Life Energy and Spirit are all Important

We have three parts that make us who we are: our physical body, our life energy and our spiritual nature. All three parts of you are important in your practice.

Your physical body is mainly just material. In the book "*Chi: Discovering Your Life Energy*" I used an analogy that likened the body to the dust pulled together by a tornado. You might say you saw a tornado, but you never really saw a tornado, you only saw the debris that it hurled around. The real tornado is that invisible force moving the wind. Like that tornado, your physical body is just the debris and material that is gathered up and held together by your life energy.

But without that material, without your physical body, none of this would work. You need a healthy body to keep practicing. If a tornado picks up a lot of heavy debris and junk, it slows down and dies. If it's made up of just pure powder and dust, it can go very fast and keep going much longer.

Your body enables you to have life energy; therefore, you are in trouble if you don't take care of your body. Your body is like the horse you ride on through life. I've seen many people who take better care of their horses than they do their own body. They take special care to make sure their horse eats only the best feed. They brush and bathe their horse, and make sure it gets the right amount of exercise. But when it comes to their own body, they treat it like junk.

We have to take care of our body the same way we would take care of a thoroughbred horse. As we raise our energy through practice, we learn to listen to the right message from our body about what it needs and what will hurt it. For example, if I eat an appropriate amount, with the right attitude, my body is happy and I can feel it. If I feed my body out of greedy desire, or feed it because somebody else says I should eat this and that, then I become the enemy of my body. Then after the deterioration of my body, my body won't serve me and will protest.

Life energy is the second part of ourselves that we need to take care of. As we said before, life energy is extremely important, although we take it for granted and forget about it most of the time. With proper training, you can grow, strengthen and develop your life energy. You can even learn how to move that energy around to accomplish things. This is called "Chi application." Some people become very good at using their life energy and applying it to martial arts and healing work.

But no matter how good you get at Chi application, you may still end up ignoring your spiritual nature. You may spend so much time healing others or practicing martial arts skill that you never take your Chi ability and apply it to the task of cleaning your own energy and connecting with your Te.

Our spiritual self is also very important. You may spend your whole life unaware of what the spiritual part of you really is, what mission it needs to accomplish in this life, and what problems it may have. If you have unresolved spiritual problems, or a mission that is required of you on the spiritual level, then you may have obstacles in reaching your Te no matter how adept you are at Chi application. Without paying attention to your spiritual nature, you may fail to learn how to navigate through the spiritual dimension of your journey and understand how it affects you.

To take care of all three parts of ourselves, body, life energy and spirit, we have to turn our mind and our sincerity back to feeling. First we learn how to feel our body again, then we work on feeling our life energy. After you can feel your own life energy, you can strengthen and purify that life energy until you can feel your own Te. During each step we are using the same tool: sincere feeling. When we work toward feeling our entire body, then our life energy, then our Te, we use our sincere feeling at progressively higher levels.

The process of moving meditation, done with sincere feeling, restores and reconnects these three parts of ourselves, repairing and harmonizing each of the three with each other. In the highest form of moving meditation, these three parts move together as one: body, life energy and Te.

Birth, Illness, Aging and Death
When you are born, you come into this dimension with a high level and integrity of life energy. But from the minute you are

born, that energy starts to decline. Because of those defects that came with your recycled energy, and because of the distractions and demands of this artificial world, you start to lose energy and that original signal inside of you starts to get weaker.

When you have a defect, artificial thinking, a debt of sin, it's like having a leaky bucket. It causes a drain on your life energy. Those defects steer us in a direction away from God, life and truth, causing us to waste or lose our life energy. This loss of life energy is what leads to illness, aging and death.

Death isn't like a final end. Death means you've lost so much life energy that you cannot hold together and vibrate in this human level dimension anymore, at least in a way that defines you as a living being.

After somebody dies, they still have a very low level of life energy. They are not fully dead. Their hair still grows, their fingernails still grow. But they don't have enough to hold everything together. We consider that they've crossed a boundary where they are no longer a living being. They can't maintain consciousness or intelligence. They can't hold onto that Te.

When you die, your energy starts to decay and fall apart. Your proteins and minerals start to breakdown. Your Chi gradually will drop down and break up into all its various pieces and parts and fall away to be recycled again for other living beings. Your Te will split off to start its journey back into that spiritual dimension, working toward its original source – God.

The path from birth to death is like a conveyor belt at a meat factory. You ride on a conveyor belt with all the other cattle at the slaughterhouse and pass through death. Death is like a meat grinder with nothing left of "you" on the other side. Once in awhile a cow wakes up and looks around and quietly steps off that conveyor belt, knowing it leads to no good. You can be like that cow if you have the right information and the right guidance on how to practice.

The good news is that those old wisdom teachings show us how to improve our life so that we can get off that conveyor belt and run the other direction. They gave us the keys on how to practice in order to find our Te. If we can practice and attain this goal, birth, death, illness and aging have less of a strangle-hold on us.

That conveyor belt governing human life moves one way, one direction only, from birth toward death. On our spiritual journey, we want to go "backwards," the opposite way. We don't want to keep traveling toward weaker and weaker life energy and ultimate death. We want to go backward so that our life energy becomes strong and pure again, like a baby. That's when you were the purest, strongest and most original.

Most people think we get better, stronger and more worthwhile as we age. Actually we are constantly declining from the moment of our birth. We decline because we get further away from that gateway, that moment when the pure Te entered this dimension and we created that single cell. If we can become pure enough to find that Te again, we can slip in and out of that gateway. The doors of birth and death are no longer locked, the conveyor belt stops.

Those old teachings give you the tools for cleaning and restoring yourself so that you can connect back and feel that Te. Because if you can connect to that Te, when you die, you can keep yourself together by holding onto that Te. By holding onto that Te, you can stay whole as you travel through that spiritual dimension on your journey back to God. You won't go through that meat grinder at the end of the conveyor belt.

Coincidentally, the same work you need to do in order to find your Te is the same type of work you need to do to stop the leaks in your bucket that drain your life energy. You can stop the continuous loss of Chi and raise your life energy level to extend the healthy, useful years in your life. That way you can practice even more. It buys you more time so that you can reach your goal of returning back to God.

The old Taoist practices that aimed for longevity weren't just so that they could enjoy a ripe old age. They were trying to extend their health and their years so that they had more time to work on strengthening their connection to Te before they died. If they could practice long enough to find their Te, then they knew they would have a better shot at real longevity – eternal life with God.

Like we said, when you are born you come into this life from that spiritual dimension. Your energy starts out strong, but immediately starts to decay and decline. It keeps declining year by year, until at some point you die and go back into that spiritual dimension. It's like a downward slope.

Although aging is inevitable in this limited dimension, your descent can be fast or slow. If you can slow that rate of decline and raise that slope, you can add more years to your life. You can boost yourself up in order to glide further. It's as if you are working to build a runway that's long enough so that your plane can take off.

Illness isn't the only thing that depletes your life energy, accidents and injury can also bring your energy down. You can be gliding along just fine, but if you get into a car accident, that can bring down your slope very abruptly and you can start aging quickly again.

By bringing your energy higher, you can see better on the spiritual level. This can help you know in advance when an obstacle is coming. It helps you avoid disasters like accidents and injury. That's why it's so important to gain the ability to feel your life energy. You want your life energy to be in harmony with everything around you so you don't collide with anything else.

We have to treat life and consciousness as solid real stuff. It changes, stretches, declines, centralizes, or strays away from the center. But if we cannot feel it, how can we nourish, protect and keep it strong?

When you lose life energy, it's like a candle flickering in the wind. As you get closer to death, it's as if the candle is flickering to the point of being blown out. That's why old people can have a weak and disoriented mind. Their energy level is getting closer to that range where they are flickering. Sometimes things make sense to them, sometimes they don't make sense. If a candle flame is flickering, ready to go out, the flame is "sick."

By the same token, if you keep your flame of life energy strong and steady, you can go back and use it to repair your energy and take care of your body.

You always want to keep your life energy strong up until it's time to leave this dimension and die. In fact you especially want to have strong and pure life energy at that moment. Strong energy at the time of your death can help you make the highest achievement.

The Highest Achievement
The reason we crave longevity is because of that piece of God inside. It remembers that we are supposed to live forever. But we have to remind ourselves that we don't want to live forever within this limited physical dimension of suffering. We want to travel back to God's dimension and live forever.

People on a spiritual journey can often work so hard to take care of their physical health in pursuit of longevity that they forget their original goal. They can forget to spend the time necessary to take care of their life energy too. Taking care of our physical health is only part of the picture; we also have to take care of our life energy.

Let's say we're on a journey, and we have to drive from New York to San Francisco. We need a good car but we also need a good driver. If you don't take care of both the car and the driver, you'll never make it. Our body is like a car we are driving, but our life energy is like the driver. Although the car is important, taking care of the driver should be our first consideration, not the other way around.

The reason you need to take care of your life energy first, is because when you reach the end of this human journey, you will need that life energy in order to survive the point where you go through death and that gateway back into the spiritual dimension.

People enjoy comparing our transformation after death to a caterpillar transforming into a butterfly. It is a beautiful imagery. But we have to remember that the same life energy inside that caterpillar is what turns into the life energy of the butterfly. If you step on that caterpillar and injure it, or if it is weak and underfed, that caterpillar won't have enough life energy to transform itself. Then guess what? No butterfly.

Different levels of life energy mean different levels of achievement at death. At the lowest level, you go through that gate and your energy is split apart and sorted back into the recycling bin, while your Te returns on its journey back to God. Whatever made up the totality of "you" is split apart and goes off in many directions.

A second level of achievement is to know in advance when you are going to die. This gives you a chance to smooth out your life, work on yourself and clean up your energy before you go. If you raise your energy high enough so that you can touch that spiritual dimension and know when you will die, this is a great advantage. It helps you resolve many issues which might otherwise hold you back after death. Spiritualized people who raise their energy this high aren't usually scared by knowing when they are going to die. They are surprisingly resolute and working hard to raise their energy even higher.

A higher level of achievement is being able to choose when you will die. You can see high enough to be able to fully resolve any spiritual issues or spiritual debts in this life well in advance of your death. You have nothing holding you in this human dimension any more. You are free to decide when you want to go.

In the old days, some Taoist and Buddhist monks made this achievement. When they got older and ready to leave, they would pick a day and a time, make an announcement to the temple, and arrange a big ceremony for everyone to attend on the chosen day. They would then climb up on a platform, sit in meditation, and at just the right time they would quietly die, leaving their body behind. That feat is evidence that they had a high enough frequency of energy that they could hold themselves completely intact as they left this world and traveled through the gateway into the spiritual dimension.

An even higher level of achievement is when you can come and go freely from that spiritual dimension whenever you choose. You are no longer tied down by this heavy physical dimension at all. You are pure and refined enough to slip in and out of that gateway between our dimension and the spiritual dimension at will.

But the highest level some of those old masters achieved is what they called "daytime ascending." They could raise their energy so high that they could dissolve even their bodies into pure energy and just vanish and turn into a "saint." You can see this sort of event recorded in the old legends or notes of this sort of master turning up from time to time in the official records.

All of this wisdom that spiritual masters have been practicing since the old days focuses on such achievements. They teach you how to handle aging and illness in the most successful way, and then how to make a smooth passage to that other dimension at your death.

Death is by far the most misunderstood part of our journey. Many people think that they will meet God when they die. That's not necessarily true. You need to meet God while you are still alive! You need to be able to morph into that butterfly while you are still alive. You must transform yourself in this life in order to connect with God. That process requires life energy. If you die before you've made that change, you won't have enough life energy to make it on the other side.

That's why it is so important in *this* lifetime to raise your energy and contact that Te inside of you.

The Importance of Te

In your Taichi moving meditation practice, you must keep going, condensing, purifying, until finally you can feel your Te. It's like going to the center of the Earth. I keep digging and digging, until I can feel the core.

Although our Te is the root of our very life, we don't own that Te. That piece of Te belongs to God. When that Net is in action, it expands and contracts. It shrinks itself to form that Te. So even though Te is created by and comes from God, when it shrinks it separates and becomes "less" than God.

When that Te comes into this dimension, Te pulls in Chi and Chi pulls in enzymes and material to make your body. If during your life, that Chi weakens, your Chi can no longer organize and hold onto that material and your body decays. At the same time, when your Chi weakens, eventually that Chi cannot hold onto the Te either. When Chi can no longer hold onto it, then the Te will detach and continue its journey to Tao, in whichever direction it is heading.

When you die and all of this material drops away and decays, if your Te is pure enough, it can return to Tao. That is why we want our mind to be able to feel and connect to Te in our practice. If we can feel and connect to our Te, then at the moment of our death we can grab hold of that Te, ride on that Te, and be pure enough to go with Te back to Tao. If we cannot do this, at the point of our death we will find our mind and Chi moving further away from Te and separating from each other.

This is why finding your Te is important. In the end, what we really want is pure Te, period. We want to be with pure Te in order to return to Tao. If we want Te, we must purify both Chi and Te so they get very clean, so they are not split apart or cracked. The cleaner Chi and Te become, the better they can hold together.

Your Te has been used many times, so has the Chi, and so has the material used to form your body. You have a history that comes imprinted on both your Te and Chi. In our own lives, we contaminate our Chi and Te even further. Since Chi and Te combine together to create the mind, this distortion of Chi and Te is what makes our mind so polluted and unreliable.

It is up to us to do whatever is necessary, struggling to purify ourselves, so that we can eliminate this contamination and distortion. By eliminating the contamination and distortion, we return back to the original feeling of what the Tao wants to do and how it moves. Then we can follow that feeling.

Wherever you train your mind to go, that is where it will lean at the time of your death. If in our lifetime we train our mind to pay more attention to law, politics, money, human relationships, or desires, it is toward those things that our mind will tend to go at the end of life. But the unfortunate truth is that all those other outward things become empty and collapse at the point of death. If you are holding onto such empty things, then when they collapse, your consciousness is left with nothing to hold onto.

Likewise, we must guard against training our mind to get stuck focusing on the physical level of our body. This is important to remember in Taichi. Why? Because in Taichi, we spend a good deal of time relearning how to feel, move, use and take care of our body the right way. This is an important first step on our journey to becoming more real. But it's important that we don't stop there. And unfortunately many people do stop there.

Let's say I'm content with focusing my utmost attention to the feeling of my physical body, my health, my Taichi form, my body's performance, the real feeling and balance of my body as it moves. If I stay there and keep training my mind to attach to my body, that body ages and dies. Then where will I be? So although it is a marker of progress to feel and move your body the right way, it is still not our ultimate goal.

Also, we can get stuck at the Chi level on this Taichi journey. Once we can feel, strengthen, flow and use our Chi, this is also a marker of great success. It can be exhilarating to use Chi for healing, martial arts and spiritual work. But so many people stop there and never develop and use that Chi toward the highest goal, of reconnecting with Te. Chi that has not reconnected with Te will drop away and keep recycling after your death, so reconnecting with Chi is not your ultimate goal either.

Here is the right way to look at our progress in moving meditation: We take care of our body and learn to feel and move the original way so we can learn how to feel the Chi. We practice feeling, strengthening and purifying our Chi so that we can use it to go deeper and feel our Te.

It's that Te that we are betting on for the highest achievement in Taichi. Without this achievement, at death the body decays and unrefined Chi falls away. But with this achievement, we are holding onto that life raft of Te which is unsinkable. So even if this big cruiser sinks, we keep traveling toward Tao.

We don't own our Chi or our body. Our physical material and our Chi were used before by somebody else, and will drop away at our death to be used again. They are temporary to us. They are like the clothes I'm wearing. Are the clothes I'm wearing "me?" No. But I am inside them, and as long as I am inside them, it's as if they are a part of me.

Is the building you are sitting in "you?" No. But because you are sitting inside of it, what happens to that building affects you. When the building you are sitting starts burning to the ground, are you going to be trapped inside of it? Watch out! You want to be able to leave that burning building and run away to safety.

Will you be trapped at your death, or able to leave? What do you want to grab onto? Don't grab onto what is temporary, fake or doomed to fall away and sink.

If you grab onto hollow prayers to God: "Oh please God, save me!" but have never been able to pray with true sincere feeling and touch that Net while you were alive, what will your chance of success be at your death? But if during your life you have practiced and prayed in such a way as to be able reach Te, and you know how to pray with a sincere mind and make that connection to God, WOW!

A normal human being cannot make this achievement through so-called knowledge and education. Knowledge is man-made. Real wisdom is infinite. Life and death are big issues. Don't try and approach them with small tools like knowledge.

<u>Go to Te Instead of Thinking</u>

That's why it is important to do real practice that leads to the ability to reconnect with Te. This ability to reconnect is far more important than any human level learning you can attain. When you touch this Net, you don't need that human knowledge because you instantly know all you need to know.

If I do correct moving meditation and purify myself so much that my mind, my feeling, my thinking, match that frequency of God, then I know everything just by touching that frequency. I automatically understand everything. I don't have to "know" or "learn" anything in the human sense. I already have it. If I want to know anything, I just touch that Net. The truth I receive from that instant communication with God far outstrips any human level knowledge or learning on this earth.

Because this Net connects everywhere and sees through everything, it's as if I suddenly can hear everybody thinking. I can see everybody and what they've already done or thought, and what they're going to do. If I can do that, do I need to learn anything? Do I need to get a degree or read books in order to know? No. So why do we worship and spend so much time chasing knowledge and degrees, thinking we can figure out our way back to heaven, rather than spending time to learn how to reconnect with our Te?

Learning is not truth. Learning and knowledge are based on man-made thinking. Man-made thinking is what keeps us traveling further away from God. If I think I'm a very educated person, I'm in trouble. That means there's a lot of someone else's fake ideas in my brain. Instead of helping me find the truth, it keeps me further away. This is why Lao Tzu says things like:

> *"Give up learning and become worry-free…"*
> *"Shut your knowledge; close the door of your cleverness."*
> *"He learns how to not need to learn,*
> *to avoid repeating others' mistakes…"*
> *"Those who know the truth possess no knowledge.*
> *Those who possess knowledge do not know the truth…"*
>   Lao Tzu, *Tao Te Ching*, Chapters 20, 52, 64 and 81

This is also what Lao Tzu tried to describe when he said:

> *"Never going outdoors, yet he knows*
> *everything under heaven.*
> *Never looking outside of the window,*
> *he can see the Tao of heaven.*
> *He who tries to act, the farther he searches,*
> *the less he knows.*
> *A saint takes no action to investigate,*
> *yet knows everything."*
> Lao Tzu, *Tao Te Ching*, Chapter 47

Some other translations quote Lao Tzu as saying: "*A Taoist can stay in the house and know the whole world.*" For so long, nobody could understand what Lao Tzu was talking about. Back then, that seemed like mysticism. But today we have better analogies. Today, you can stay inside your hotel room with the shades drawn, your laptop connected to the Internet, have access to a television and a cell phone, and you can know what's going on just about anywhere else in the world. You can stay inside your room and know everything! But if you disconnect from that digital information network, then you can't access that information anymore. It's the same way with Tao. If you can connect to that Network, you can stay wherever you are and know everything.

What Lao Tzu was talking about was connecting to that network of universal energy in order to know everything you need to know. He tried to say that if you can connect to your Te, you don't need to go anywhere to know anything and everything in the whole universe. This is why Lao Tzu also says, "The further you go, the less you know." That means that the further you stray from the signal of your own Te, the further you are from knowing the truth. The more you look to outside answers, instead of to that internal connection to God, whatever you "know" or learn has little value in the end and may actually draw you even further from the truth.

Truth means true feeling. If we can access true feeling, we can know the truth. Truth means that when I'm faced with a need to know something, I bypass all my human knowledge and forget about it. Instead, I let that "need to know" hit my Te, and go to God. What I feel in my Te is a true answer. That's real truth. If instead I take a "short cut" and send my man-made question to my brain, where it goes to the data-bank of my knowledge, and then I concoct a man-made answer based on my data and opinions, that answer is fake.

My greatest hope is to someday see all human beings get rid of and ignore the collective nonsense that we revere as our knowledge, and let that system collapse. If we all ignored what we think, and what we think we "know," and instead did everything only by asking the Te, asking our true feeling, then the whole world would be a much better place to live.

Our thinking, our smartness, our intellectual knowledge is not Te anymore. It's just pollution we've acquired. So in respect to our returning to our origin, the smarter I get, the further away I go. The highest achievement is when you bring your life energy and merge once again back to the net of God so that you think the way

God thinks, you feel what God feels, you see the way God sees, and you live how God lives. That's called eternity. You don't separate yourself from God. It is when we rely on our own thinking that we humans try to separate from God.

To truly understand the Tao, the way of God, we have to qualify ourselves. How? By giving up all our accumulated artificial knowledge and ideas, and then touching the true feeling of life energy so we can reach that piece of God inside. How do we accomplish this? By "reduction."

The Way Back to God is by Reduction
The key to changing and qualifying ourselves is through what Lao Tzu calls reduction.

> *"In the pursuit of studying world affairs,*
> *every day your knowledge accumulates.*
> *In the pursuit of Tao, every day you abandon.*
> *You abandon more — you reduce......"*
> Lao Tzu, *Tao Te Ching*, Chapter 48

"Abandon" or "reduce" means we get rid of everything that is blocking our ability to feel and experience our pure life energy. That means everything that points us outward and away from Te.

One of Buddha's greatest teachings was the Diamond Sutra. In the Diamond Sutra, Buddha was talking about the ultimate pure energy of God both inside of us and permeating the entire universe. A diamond is different from any other material on earth. It is so clear you can see right through it. Yet it is so hard, it can cut through anything else. It is so precious, so pure, so clear and so valuable, there is nothing else like it in the whole world.

Buddha was trying to tell us that that piece of God inside of us is like a diamond. Since Buddha was a prince, he had once lived in great wealth and privilege. He was one of the few people in those days fortunate enough to have likely seen and held a real diamond.

We all have that piece of diamond inside of us, but it is like buried treasure. We have to find it. But how can we do that? We find that diamond by getting rid of everything that is "not-diamond."

Let's say somebody told me that there was a priceless 30-carat diamond hidden in my messy garage, how would I go about finding it? I would go out to my garage and pick up every piece of junk and carefully examine it. "Is this a diamond? Does it contain a diamond? Is it perfectly clear? Can it cut through anything? No!" Everything that was not a diamond would be thrown out onto the driveway. Sometimes I might have to stop awhile and think carefully. "Hmmm...this piece of aluminum is hard and shiny, just like a diamond. But it's not clear and it can't cut through everything else. Out it goes!" I would keep going, keep discarding each item, until finally, I found that priceless diamond. I found that diamond by the process of "reduction."

Likewise, in our practice and lifestyle, we reduce by identifying and burning off impurities and relying less and less on those things that are artificial. We use our meditation time to throw away and ignore everything inside and outside of us that is not that diamond, that pure life energy. We stop adding to and feeding the artificial layers in our life, and instead divert our energy back toward what is real. We use the power of sincere feeling to burn through all the layers of insulation that hide that precious diamond inside of us.

The way to truth is to get rid of non-truth. All you need is to see a diamond once. Then you know the truth. Once you see even a tiny little piece of diamond, nobody can show you anything outside of a diamond and convince you it's a diamond.

Burning off our impurity and getting rid of non-truth can sound really difficult and complicated. Not true! It is during this journey that we rely on faith. Faith will carry us along on this journey and help us with the answers we need. All the answers are inside of us, inside of our Te – including the answers we need to keep making progress toward our goal. The more progress we make, the more we can hear that signal that keeps us going in the right direction. As long as we keep working toward that diamond with sincerity, we will keep making progress.

Although we previously compared the work of reaching our Te to digging through rock to find the core of the Earth, a better way to look at it is this: Instead of "dig, dig, dig," we learn to "ignore, ignore, ignore." The *T'ai Chi Classics* talk about "yielding," and the *Tao Te Ching* says "reduce" or emphasizes "weakness." It all means "give up, give up, give up," until you finally get there. You let go in order to make progress. Reduction and return means you unload all the burden of all the artificial everything in this world, then you can return to that Net and become so powerful.

What's an example of reduction? What are we trying to reduce? We are trying to reduce nonsense. Each time irrelevant issues come into our thinking, we know we are contaminated. Then we know we're not in good shape. We proudly rely on our "common sense" to approach Tao – but we forget that our common sense is nonsense with respect to God. We have to jump out of our nonsense first.

This is why moving meditation helps us with reduction. We practice reduction in Taichi by practicing to reduce nonsense. I tell my students, "When you move forward, there is nothing but forward." If I do Taichi and I want to move forward, but then as I move forward I discover that I'm thinking about all kinds of other issues, like: "I want to push somebody," "I don't know why I want to move forward," "I hate you," "I wonder if my form looks good," "I'm hungry." All of these thoughts are not about moving forward.

Forward means nothing but forward! Anything else is irrelevant. Just feel and move forward, reducing any distraction that is not about moving forward. This is the practice by which you can upgrade yourself closer to the original way your energy is supposed to be. Until we make that upgrade, we are just a part of this nonsense on earth. Our signal remains weak and confused by all the nonsense inside of us. If we can reduce that nonsense inside of us, then we can penetrate and see the eternal reality.

So when I have nonsense that comes into my brain, that's a bad sign. Right away I want to reduce that. It is too much of a burden and drain on my life energy. Not only does nonsense point me away from Te, it attracts and feeds that contamination. Dump it.

Small children are much less contaminated than we are. Little kids don't have reasons when they play. They just say, "I like to do this." "I don't like this." "I don't like you." They don't need a reason. Their brains aren't spinning in three directions at once. That's a sign that their energy is much purer than an adult's. One day when your little son or daughter starts to give you excuses and reasons for why they are doing something, you know your kid is now contaminated with man-made nonsense in his or her head. Before that, they just did what they wanted to from following that original energy, with no reason.

We are all contaminated and full of nonsense because we are in this dimension. This lifetime is a chance for each of us to clean up our act, to move forward, to raise the frequency of our energy. But to do that, we aren't looking to "gain" anything on this spiritual journey. We don't "get" spiritualized. Everybody is already spiritualized, we just "get" polluted and "gain" contamination. We do not get to Tao by gaining something. The more we "gain" the more burdens in our mind and the more problems we have. We were born spiritualized, but we've become non-spiritualized by what we've gained.

We get to Tao by reducing so much that all we have left is Te. We don't need to gain or acquire Te. We reduce what's not real in order to find it. We already have it. In a certain play on written characters, "Te" can mean "gain" in Chinese. Only when you find your Te can you truly "gain" anything of true value. If you look anywhere else beside your Te for gain, you lose.

We're working to find what we already have. And we find it by losing what is not real — by reduction. That's why when the old monks joined the temple, they would shave their head and give up all their belongings. This symbolized that from now on, they were going to drop everything in order to find that Te.

The Most Powerful Person

Many of today's self-help and spiritual teachings extol the virtues of using your mental or spiritual powers to get what you want. They want you to buy their spiritual teachings so that you can learn how to gain health, gain wealth, gain friends, gain knowledge, gain happiness, and otherwise add things to your human life. You don't often hear of spiritual teachings in today's modern world talking about reduction. They miss the highest truth, which is this: *"The most powerful person in the world is the one who needs the least."*

Let's say we each decide that we are going to travel from here to France on a trip. In order to go to France, you pack four trunks full of fashionable clothes and accessories. Then you hire a kennel to watch your purebred dog, reserve a limousine to take you to your private jet at the airport. Meanwhile you call your doctor to refill three prescriptions and hire a private nurse to come along with you to administer your medication on the trip. You call your two managers that you rely on to run your many businesses and tell them that they must drop everything and come with you to France so you can manage your affairs while you are abroad.

To the rest of the world, all of this makes it sound like you are a very wealthy and powerful person. In actuality, you are very weak and dependent. Why? You are weak because without your reliance on all these many outside things, you would not be able to go to France.

Now let's say that on my trip to France, I simply stick a toothbrush in my pocket and walk out my door without need for any other preparation. I am very powerful indeed! I am more powerful than you! Why? Because I know that I will have everything I need when I have the power and ability to rely on nothing else but God.

Why in the ancient temples did Buddhist and Tao monks have nothing? They were trying as hard as possible to burn off all the nonsense of the artificial world in order to find that Te inside. They were also learning and living the important lesson that the richest person in the world is the person who needs the least.

Study the old days how monks, be they Buddhists, Taoists or Christians, had no possessions. Jesus had no possessions. That type of lifestyle encourages you to connect to God so much that you are able you to defy anything "not God" like gold, silver, power, reputation or property. Those old monks knew that when you rely on or bow to those fake systems, you cannot connect to God. That's why the old discipline in the temple included "no possessions."

Furthermore, these wandering monks did their healing and helping work without reward. They didn't rely on earning money for their spiritual service. To do that would put what is real at the service of what is fake.

Jesus healed and raised people from the dead. How much did he charge for that? He might get some food from the family afterwards who invited him to stay for dinner. Everything he did was free. Conversely, let's think what would happen if somebody in our fake world could actually cure people no matter what their disease, or raise somebody from the dead. How much would a hospital charge for such a service?

This human society, this artificial society, is a place of suffering and sin. It is a destiny of disaster. When humans separate themselves from God, the lie starts. The only way to solve that lie is another lie. Once that cycle starts, you can never get out. So the training of that old temple life meant that those monks had to write themselves off from this human society. In the temple, you are no longer a participant in such human level institutions built on lies. When you enter the temple, you are entering God's kingdom, God's truth.

After the monks trained inside the temple to rely on God, it wasn't enough. They were forced to leave the temple and to go out and practice this way of living within human society. They had to prove that they could maintain that connection to God even when they left the temple and went to the city. It was their test. Could they do it? Could they survive? Could they keep their reliance on God alone, and not fall back into those fake systems? So for a time, each monk was sent out to wander.

In the old days, such wandering monks were not allowed to earn money or purchase things because they were not allowed to participate in artificial society. They lived by the truth that this earth belongs to everyone. The only possessions they had were their robe, their walking staff and their begging bowl. The only thing they needed from the outside was food, and perhaps some shelter if it was cold.

In God's truth, there is no such thing as "your food" or "my food." So they walked through town with their begging bowl and asked: "Do you have any spare food?"

Begging for food isn't so simple. These monks also had to learn how to beg for food without a profit mind. They'd take whatever they got, and couldn't save any for later. They learned to give their help from sharing and passion only, unaffected by how they were fed or treated by others.

Let's say you are a monk out begging for food and somebody spits on you and says, "No food for you! Get out of here you filthy bald-headed monk!" But the next day, that same person comes to you for healing. You are not allowed to say no. You cannot say to yourself, "Ha! Now I'll teach this guy a lesson on why he should be nice to monks! I'll refuse to heal him." If you respond to this person from any idea that you cooked up artificially in your mind to teach him what you think he needs to learn, that means you worship the wrong God. No matter how well or how badly he has treated you, you must go to God and let God be in charge of whether or not he will be healed, with no bias. Why? Because as a monk, you live in God's power and this is all up to God.

These are just some of the reasons why that training in the old days included such practices. They used that practice to develop their power of connection to God. This goes back to that true wisdom, "The most powerful person is the one who needs the least."

This artificial world thrives on need. In this fake world of hospitals, lawyers, politics and insurance, they love people who have lots of trouble and who need their services. When you need them, they can control you and profit from you.

But when you don't need anything, you are so wealthy! You don't need to engage with those artificial hijacked systems! They have no power over you! Those who run those evil and fake systems hate people who are content, need nothing, and neither cause nor experience trouble.

Those old monks knew the truth: the only thing they needed was God. They knew that the human world split off from God into a lie. They wanted to steer their disciples away from the lie and toward the truth.

Of course, any human system, even a temple, has sin. Eventually that temple system crumbled down and there are few such temples left. Today, many of the old rituals, like begging or shaved heads, remain intact in some places, but unfortunately, much of the real wisdom behind the old rituals is gone.

Today we can learn from what those old monks tried to do and apply it to our own practice. Do we have to shave our head and go begging? No. It's not necessary to become a wandering monk. We can simply learn to reduce our need for artificial systems and ideas, and strengthen our connection to God. This is another way of practice in which we qualify ourselves to feel the way of Tao.

Ultimately, reducing your sense of need is a way to reduce the power of evil over you. That evil power knows what we want and can use that to trap us. As a simple example, I need food and evil knows it. That's why evil can zero in on food and manipulate our food production, distribution and our access to food in order to make us slaves. But if I don't need food, there is no way for those outside forces to control me.

Did you know that in the old days there were monks who achieved such a high level that they didn't even need to eat food to survive? Such ability is rarely seen anymore, since those old masters have long since died out.

One famous Taichi master in the 20th Century, Cheng Man Ching, was old enough to have actually met one of these masters. He invited this master to his house to live for awhile. Cheng Man Ching asked him why he never ate food. The old master told Cheng that he ate once every year when heaven's gate opened.

One day, while he was staying with Cheng Man Ching, he told Cheng, "Heaven's gate is open. I can eat for the next twenty-four hours." He told Cheng to go get him one hundred bean-stuffed steamed buns and a gallon of wine. Cheng did so, and when he brought them back, the old master sat down and slowly ate through every single bun. At the end of twenty-four hours, the master stood up and said, "Heaven's gate is shut now. I'll eat again next year."

Cheng Man Ching was a highly achieved Taichi master, so he tried to be like this old master too. He went for a couple weeks without food, but became weak and sick and eventually had to eat. But he achieved enough in his lifetime to actually meet one of these old masters in person.

Go to God with "No Strings Attached"

When you go to God, go with "no strings attached." You must contact that Te with no agenda in order to reach the frequency of God or it won't work and you will end up landing short.

This means you cannot go to God for a reward or gift or favor. This includes going to God because you want honor in heaven, or because you want the power to heal the world, or you want a reward after death, or because you want a new car, a new spouse or an ice cream cone. No! You just go to God purely for the sake of connecting to God. Just to know God is a privilege and a blessing. It is enough.

Your approach should be that you want to be with God for no reason. You have to want to be with God for no reason and at any cost.

Unfortunately, this means that if you are sick and want to be with God in order to feel better, you have the wrong motivation and will fall short. If you want to be with God so your suffering will go away, you won't make it. This is why those old churches had people go to priests who would pray for them. In theory, the priest could do a better job to connect with God on their behalf, because he could stay detached and calm. He could approach God with no agenda, because he wasn't the one suffering. Then, if God chose to send a message of healing and help, the priest could broadcast that power of God out toward those who needed it.

Any time you go to God with a desire or strings attached, you risk failure to reach the high frequency needed to reach the one true God. It is tricky, because even when you think you have no reason, you can even make wanting to connect with God a selfish ambition or a point of spiritual pride or personal gain. The best approach and best attitude to hold is that you just want to be clean and connect, that's all. Truthfulness, honesty, faith, seeing things clearly, humbleness, these are the most important attributes that will raise your frequency.

Sometimes our ideas about God are a barrier. When Jesus talked about God as "our Father," he gave us a great analogy. After all, God is the source of our life and we are God's offspring. But you have to be very careful when you use that same approach toward God. While it's good to approach God with the humility, sincerity and innocence of a child, when we try to treat God like a Father or a Mother, this can prove to be a mistake. That can bring your energy down. You were raised in this human world, and our human ideas of fathers and mothers and how they treat their children can be very tarnished.

Let's say when you grew up that every time you cried and made trouble, your mother gave you a cookie or candy to keep you quiet. You learned that if you cry and cause trouble, you'll get relief or attention. Unknowingly, when you approach God, you come with that same attitude: you cry for what you want until you get relief. You will fail to reach that ultimate frequency and not even understand why, because this conditioned way of thinking controls you so completely. We've already talked about the error that can seep in when we see God as a strict father figure monitoring our morals. All of our ideas about how fathers and mothers act come from this limited world. If we really had any idea how good fathers and mothers act, we wouldn't have so many broken homes, so much child abuse and so many arguments over proper child-rearing philosophies.

To reach the frequency of God in prayer requires the utmost purity. We have to dump all of our worldly ideas and comparisons.

Reaching the frequency of God in prayer is one reason why those old teachings taught that we should reduce our desires. If you have a desire, it's like a dark cloud blocking your way to Tao. Your sincerity, letting go and giving up such desires makes you "open." Once you have desire, you close down again. As soon as you can be with God, everything will be taken care of. But don't go there with that desire.

The way to Tao is by reduction, especially in prayer. Even if you are sick, don't think about being sick, just accept it, ignore it, and let the issue go. There is no "*sick*," no "*broke*," only "*give up, give up, give up*," until there is nothing more to give up. Carefully keep going and giving up until all self is gone. At some point, like Lao Tzu, you will find that even when self is gone, there is something still there.

Those who believe in miracles worship the wrong God. Why? What is a miracle? The first person to see an airplane fly thought it was a miracle. It wasn't a miracle; it was simply something that was not yet widely understood. Everything comes from and is a part of that network of God, so everything is a miracle. And if everything is a miracle, then there are no miracles.

If you are waiting for a miracle, then you worship the wrong god. Why not just worship God? Worshipping the wrong god equals worshipping the devil. Worshipping a small "god" equals worshipping the devil too. You need to constantly remind yourself, "I only want the ultimate God, the eternal conscious power of everything." If you hold onto that, then all that other stuff moves out of the way.

Still, many people pray for what they call a "miracle." If you look too hard for miracles, manipulative people or even that dark force can use "miracles" to trick you. That's why in the Catholic Church the Vatican has to give its verification as to what is a real miracle. Over many centuries, they've learned that miracles can be fake or delude many people toward the wrong direction.

A fake miracle may include somebody who shows you they can do spiritual reading, or they can do healing. Why? It can take a long time to see whether a spiritual reading or healing is truly of real and lasting value and based on the power of God. We are easily mesmerized by false words and temporary comfort.

Attracting people's sincerity through performing miracles is very cruel, because it exploits the most valuable thing a person has: their desire for and trust in God. If you sincerely believe in something, that's like a seed you are planting. If you plant that seed and believe in that miracle no matter what or where it comes from, and then base your journey on seeking more miracles, then you plant a seed in evil.

A person looking for miracles is like a child looking for Santa. This doesn't just apply to religious people. Scientific people have their own version of Santa, like when they believe that technology will solve all of our problems and will save us in the end.

Yes, we grown-ups want to believe in "Santa" stories too. But going to God for a miracle as if God were Santa, is going with a string attached to your prayer. That string only holds you down.

Prayer is Like Launching a Rocket

Keep trying to go directly to God to connect, even if it takes 10,000 tries. Keep going, because maybe one time you'll make it.

Do you know how a rocket works? A rocket has to build up enough velocity so that it breaks through our atmosphere and "falls off" the earth. If a rocket is not launched high enough, it will simply fall back down to earth. The rocket has to go just high enough so that when it starts to fall back down it keeps on falling into space. Prayer is like that. You keep going, keep working at it and one day you make it.

Even if you have a good heart, if you go a little bit in the wrong direction you will fail. We launch our rocket and try to connect to God, but the minute we try, wrong thinking intrudes: "Master Liao's teaching is too hard," "Maybe there is no God to reach," "I can't think today," "How did he say I should do this?" "After practice, I'm going to order a pizza." "Blah, blah, blah…" Your mind is full of garbage from negative energy trying to stop you. That's like gravity trying to pull us back down to earth. Just don't pay any attention to that nonsense. Don't fight with it either or you will only feed it. Keep ignoring it and letting it go.

Back to that question, "Why does prayer sometimes work and sometimes not?" The answer is whether you can transmit on the right frequency, and what the content of your transmission is. In other words, it depends both on how pure the person sending the prayer is, and how pure the prayer itself is. If your prayer has an un-genuine, impure, contaminated purpose, then when your prayer or meditation touches that Net, it's just noisy. That noisy message can never be delivered to that highest frequency of God.

What's worse is that prayer can fail to reach God, but be picked up by that spiritual dimension. You try to call God on the phone, but it's as if you reach the Mafia instead. "Oh, okay, you need more money and happiness in your life, here you go!" You may receive a so-called "answer" to your prayer, but that answer may be from the wrong place or carry a price-tag that you don't want to be forced to pay back. Remember, if those outside powers know what you want they can manipulate you.

Never consider prayer as just using our low-level thinking and desire to say to God, "Give me something please…" At best that is wishful thinking. At worst, it is asking for trouble.

If your desire is to return and connect, that's a good desire. If my desire is to follow true original feeling, that is a good desire. These are good desires because you are going in the right direction. Going to God just for the "heck of it" with no desire is best of all. This way, you have a better chance of launching your rocket free and clear.

Taichi moving meditation is about preparing a person to have that ability to connect and communicate and reach the highest level. Before we make a prayer, we have to go through this training to ready ourselves. When your energy is high enough so that you can broadcast a powerful clear and pure message, then you qualify yourself to deliver a prayer to that ultimate God with no misdirection.

Anyone who has utmost sincerity has direct access. In Tao meditation we develop that sincerity and concentration by focusing on a point in the center of our lower stomach called the Dan Tian. Concentrating on the Dan Tian is a tool we use to develop that power to reach God with full sincerity of heart, soul, body and mind. It's how we learn to launch that rocket. (This critical practice is described and demonstrated on DVDs available from www.taichitaocenter.com)

Stop Negative Thinking Early and Quickly
Lao Tzu said a journey of 1,000 miles begins with one step. Jesus said from a tiny seed grows a big tree. While these are important phrases about faith, these truths also apply when you are going in the wrong direction. A journey of a thousand miles in the wrong direction starts with a single step too! A field full of weeds starts with a single seed too.

That's why in our practice and daily lives we observe our thoughts, words and behavior. If we catch ourselves heading in the wrong direction we stop and correct this immediately. Otherwise that small mistake can take us far off course.

If you are steering a big ship from Canada to Norway, you can make it if you keep your ship steering in the right direction. But if you veer even one inch off course, that can be a big mistake. You might not notice it at first, and you'll still think you are heading towards Norway. But after a few hundred miles at sea, what started as a one-inch mistake can send you hundreds or even thousands of miles off course over time. You can wind up in Spain instead, or crash your boat into the icy rocks of the North Sea.

> *"Plan for difficulties while the
> situation is still simple to solve.
> Act on big things while they are still small.
> In the universe, difficult things start out easy.
> In the universe, large things arise from the small."*
> Lao Tzu, *Tao Te Ching*, Chapter 63

You have to learn to identify when a small lie enters your mind and cut it off right there, otherwise it can grow very big. One lie has a tendency to bring more lies. One negative thought can breed many more. If you only have one, two or three little monkeys clawing on you, you can probably shoo them away and say "Hey, don't come back." But if you don't get rid of those three little monkeys, pretty soon you'll have 300 monkeys grabbing hold of you. Then what can you do? They will eat you alive.

Pollution is not just bad when it's visible or in large amounts. A colorless, odorless gas in the air can kill you. One tiny virus can get you very sick, and that virus can multiply so fast. Likewise, to have a big horrible idea, you just need to start with a little bad idea. That bad idea is like a virus. It can multiply and be very contagious!

The Yellow Emperor's Classic of Internal Medicine says the best healer stops the illness before his patient even gets sick. Those old healers knew that if an illness goes deeper and deeper, it gets worse and harder to stop. If it gets to your kidneys, you are in critical condition. That's why it is important to stop an illness at the very first symptom, or better yet, prevent the illness altogether. It's the same with negative thinking.

Do you ever see how firemen stop a wildfire? If a patch of forest or a block of houses starts on fire, they will tear down a whole section of forest, or a whole house at the leading edge of the fire, even if it's not burning. Why? So the fire has nothing to grab hold of and no way to spread.

Negative thinking and lies feed on our artificial thoughts, so we can learn how to remove what feeds them before they grow and spread. We can be like those firemen and remove the fuel for those negative thoughts so they can be snuffed out.

Moving meditation teaches us how to quiet our mind and focus on what's true and real instead of on the lies and negativity in our head. Through meditation, we simply stop feeding the lies. We don't allow ourselves to get lost in the stream of contaminated thinking.

The way to get rid of bad energy is to first fill those cavities inside of you with good stuff like sincerity, gratefulness, good deeds, kind words, moving meditation, and Tao. Secondly, don't feed the bad stuff.

In our lifestyle we can learn what feeds the contamination in our mind and in our energy, and reduce and remove those things, if possible. That's why Buddha used to tell his disciples, "Can you see no evil? Hear no evil? Speak no evil?" He was teaching them to keep their mind pure and not allow even the seed of negative thought into their mind. He was telling them, "Don't feed the bad stuff!"

There was a monk in Thailand who adopted an orphaned baby tiger. From the beginning, he fed the baby tiger only cooked meat that was boiled so that there was no longer any blood in the meat. That tiger never attacked any human or animal because it never learned to crave blood. That tiger never associated the smell of living flesh with food.

We can use that same principle to help transform what is harmful and dangerous inside of us. If we carry bad energy or bad habits of meanness, cruelty, violence, lies, lust, selfishness, self-pity, fear, or any such negative signal, the best thing we can do is starve it out by boring it to death and not feeding it what it wants. If we do not feed and entertain it, eventually it will leave us. But if we feed those things, or allow them to take over and entertain themselves by making us think and do bad things, they will grow to dominate and devour us.

In our daily life, there are things we can do to bring what is off-balance back into balance. If your bad energy likes cruelty and hurting people, burn it off by starving it. Do not feed it cruelty or opportunities to hurt people. Don't read or watch stories about cruelty and hurting people. Don't listen to music about cruelty and hurting people. Don't allow thoughts about cruelty and hurting people. Use the power of your Te to stay kind and calm. Eventually, that cruel energy will get bored and want to leave.

I keep saying clean yourself, but it's better to say "qualify" yourself. We have to earn this. If we don't starve out and reduce the negative thoughts and energy inside of us, and we continue to feed what isn't true, then our temperature is not hot enough, our aim is not precise enough, our concentration is not strong enough and we cannot reach God.

Kindness Means Don't Judge

We can get those small seeds of lies by the most innocent activity. Let's say we are reading the news about some celebrity having an affair, and we judge, "Oh, he's horrible!" That's enough. That small idea lets other negative ideas in. Pretty soon we find ourselves thinking of other people we disapprove of and how horrible they are. A seed for negative thought can appear so innocent. You could be watching television and make what seems to be a positive judgment: "Gee, those models are so beautiful!" But soon you find yourself thinking, "I am so ugly. Life is so unfair. Why can't I be like those models on television?"

Judging things as good or evil usually takes place in our artificial mind. This is blockage. We are educated from the time we are small children to see and interpret things in specific limited ways. Judging somebody else's behavior as a "sin" is blockage. Judging somebody else as "good" can also be a blockage. Remember, we cannot see a person's inner nature, so we don't really know.

Lao Tzu says he values "kindness." But what does kindness really mean? Is it merely acting like a nice guy on the outside? No. Kindness means "don't judge." Every person has their own journey back to Tao. Each person has different spiritual coatings, different karma, different suffering to go through. Remember that every being has a soul and is therefore equal before Tao.

Why do all those successful bankers, lawyers and businessmen like to look down and beat up on those prostitute women who sell their body for sex? Those women are usually poor and forced into that situation. How can those men judge? Many times in their profession those men are doing the same thing, only worse.

Every day is judgment day and everybody has their own judgment. Do not worry, the universal network of Tao registers every thought and action, and in the end, all things are known by God. That balancing force will prevail.

If you see something you interpret as evil or bad, just stay humble and be grateful for your own path and keep going. When you are practicing, you let go of notions like good and evil. You don't judge and you don't care. If you experience a thought that tells you, "this is good" or "this is bad," then you are blocked.

If you say, "this is bad," then evil knows to come and play something opposite of what you think is bad in order to fool you. If you say, "This is good" then evil comes to mimic the very thing you think is good in order to fool you. Stay neutral. After all, God came before all of that, before "good and evil." Good and evil are both the offspring of God.

We can all look around the world and see that it is a very troubled and confused place with lots of evil. Admit to yourself that you are swimming in a sewer. You are. You are part of the sewer. But you get nowhere if you are so busy saying: "Oh, look at that rat! Ick! What just stuck to me? Oh, this stinks. It's suffering." Of course! You are in a sewer. Stop wasting time! Quit looking at the garbage all around you, and instead keep looking for the light and the way out.

Every day we think wrong thoughts. Every day we make mistakes — every second! That's why we want to be in Tao. We want to find Tao because every day the devil constantly assaults and attacks us.

However, even though we are under constant assault by evil, you cannot blame your sin and suffering on the darkness. It is the nature of darkness to try and cling to you, weaken you by draining your energy, and to try and come into your mind. We must realize and accept that at this point in our journey. You have to live in such a way that you can make your Te strong enough to rise above the darkness, to push it out, to endure the suffering and persevere toward Tao. Such effort makes your Te stronger.

The problem is that darkness colors our mind. It affects how we see and interpret everything around us. To illustrate this, there is an old story about a great scholar who lived in ancient China. Everyone considered him the most brilliant and educated man in the nation. However, at that time, there was also a very old and wise monk who lived in a mountain temple near the scholar's village. Every time the scholar was honored at yet another feast in the village below, the monk stayed at the temple and simply shrugged his shoulders as if he didn't care.

The scholar noticed that this monk never attended his feasts and did not offer any respect to him, so he went up to the mountain temple to challenge the monk. "Why do you not honor me? Everyone considers my accomplishments worthy of praise, and my education is most superior. What do you know compared to me?"

The monk replied, "I know nothing, but I know meditation."

The scholar laughed, "Ha! What is meditation? You know meditation, big deal."

The monk said, "You can learn quite a bit by meditating. Let's try meditating together and see what happens." The scholar nodded and took the challenge.

So they each sat on a cushion across from each other and meditated. After awhile, the monk asked the scholar, "Now that you have meditated, open your eyes and tell me what you see."

The scholar opened his eyes and looked around him. He saw a dirty, dusty and crumbling temple. When he looked at the monk, he saw a weathered and wrinkled old man with brown skin sitting like a lump with his tattered brown robe draped around him. The monk looked exactly like a piece of dung. The scholar said, "What I see is dust and decay all around me. When I look at you, I see a wrinkled fat brown lump sitting there. You look exactly like a piece of cow dung! Ah! I see now. The world is nothing but dirt and refuse."

The monk nodded knowingly. Then the monk opened his eyes and carefully looked at the scholar. The scholar asked him, "So what do you see when you look at me?"

The monk said, "What I see is that you look like a golden shining Buddha!"

The scholar beamed with pride. He bowed to the monk, and left the temple telling everyone, "See! The monk respects me after all. He meditated and told me I am like a golden shining Buddha!" The scholar went around the whole town telling his story, bragging about how the monk looked like cow dung while he was a golden and shining Buddha.

Now this scholar had an older sister who was also very intelligent and well educated. In those days, women were never acknowledged as scholars, so the sister stayed and studied privately at home. Word of what happened between her brother and the monk traveled fast around town, and the news got back to her before the scholar returned home.

When he walked into the gates, his sister ran out to meet him shaking her finger at him and crying: "You fool! That monk is much smarter than you. He just made you look like an idiot and you didn't even realize it."

The scholar replied, "What do you mean? After my meditation showed me that the world was dung and garbage, that monk honored me as superior to him! He told me that after he meditated, he could see that I was a bright and shining Buddha!"

His sister scolded him and said, "You idiot! He is a very old and wise monk. He was trying to teach you that when your inside is all dirty, all you see around you is dirt. When your inside is totally clean, then everything you see is like a golden shining Buddha. He just embarrassed you, and you are so stupid, you don't even know it."

The scholar instantly felt very humble and ashamed when he realized his mistake. The next day he went back to the same old monk on his knees and begged the monk to accept him as a disciple.

So when you see all the bad in everyone else around you, and see evil everywhere, it is because you have contamination inside. For example, if all you can think of is sex, and when you look at others, you continually see sex or judge others based on sexual sin or gossip about sex, what that really means is that inside you is contamination related to sex, or maybe you have negative energy attached to you that likes to feed on thoughts of sex.

When we let our negative thinking continue, it can dominate us and affect our behavior. If negative thoughts can dominate your mind and actions, then by definition, you are serving something other than God. And when you serve and worship the wrong God, you know the price you have to pay. Punishment comes of itself because your energy will sink lower and you will head in the wrong direction – away from the true God.

Remember Not to Worship the Wrong God
It's so very easy to believe in the wrong God. We can worship and follow the wrong God without even knowing it! After all, nobody wants to believe in the wrong God. Nobody intends to. If I knew I was worshipping the wrong God I would change right away. But most people don't know when they are worshipping the wrong God.

Let's say I am a man in a typical American family. I'm an advertising executive and have a nice, clean suburban home in a friendly neighborhood. I pray, go to church on Sundays and donate to charity. I'm a church deacon and my daughter even becomes a missionary. It may appear that I have a very spiritualized life, but in reality I worship many gods. Most of what I do, I do because my reputation as a nice and successful guy is important to me. Most of my choices are made first and foremost for the benefit of my family. In my job I talk eloquently, because I worship language and what it can do more than the true meaning behind the words. I worship money, law, science, and logic every day. I believe in those gods without knowing it as I automatically rely on and turn to those gods first in my day to day affairs. I don't intend to worship the wrong gods; it's just that this is how I've learned to live. I've been taught that this is how "good" people behave, so I follow that formula.

That's why Lao Tzu says that the more you accumulate knowledge the more you stay away from Tao. Knowledge is working like an insulator. Knowledge includes the fake culture and values we adhere to in the absence of a real connection with God.

As human beings we have our human kingdom. But our human kingdom has many other kingdoms within it. To a biologist, his or her kingdom is biology and the terms and rules of that artificial understanding of biology. To little kids, their kingdom is make believe, toys and all the trappings of childhood. Females often have certain interests, wardrobes and ways of interacting with each other that make up a female kingdom. Males have a male kingdom. A lawyer's kingdom is that crazy collection of laws and arguments and court procedures. Everything in a lawyer's kingdom makes sense to a lawyer, even if it makes no sense to the rest of us. For people who are in finance, the only things that make sense to them are numbers and values. Likewise scientists, mechanics, teachers, everybody has their own kingdom. Different countries are like different kingdoms. Certain behavior, food and art are popular in one country, but not in another.

All of these different professions, people and cultures believe and follow the rules governing those kingdoms. These different "kingdoms" are simply different forms of acquired knowledge. But they seep into our mind and our lives so deeply, they become like reality to us. In that way, by considering them real, it's as if we worship the wrong god. We follow the rules and laws of each "kingdom," rather than following the spontaneous and sincere feeling of life energy inside of us.

When you step outside of these human kingdoms and get rid of false knowledge and human rules, you can learn to feel that Net. But even as you get closer to that Net, there are still many obstacles. Why? On our journey toward the true God, we will go through that spiritual dimension at some point. Those beings and energies in the spiritual world — ghosts, "gods," evil entities, angels —they all have their own kingdoms and rules too. If you get enchanted and sidetracked by one of those spiritual kingdoms, you might end up wrongly thinking that you've reached the true God and end up staying there.

The type of thinking, the type of contamination, the type of "gods" you worship in this human kingdom can influence how and where you get sidetracked in that spiritual dimension. We tend to get sidetracked by those that match-up or resemble our history or artificial ideas. This is another reason why it's so important to burn off and shed our impurity and wrong thinking.

I always say, "You are what makes sense to you." What does this mean? It means that if you observe carefully, you can see the nature of a person's spiritual history and their energy coating. They will be drawn to what matches it.

For example, if a part of your energy was used before by a monk living in a Buddhist "kingdom," getting your head shaved might appeal to you. You might be drawn to Buddhist art, Buddhist writings, or travel to Buddhist countries. You don't know why, but you just like anything Buddhist.

What this also means, however, is that when you touch that spiritual dimension, spiritual beings with a Buddhist-type message will appeal more to you. You may end up meeting spiritual beings that also have a long history in Buddhism. But what you don't know is that they may have been Buddhist monks who failed to reach the ultimate God. They landed short in that spiritual dimension and may even be headed the wrong direction now. But because you are automatically drawn to anything "Buddhist," you could be fooled into thinking they are the true God. See how tricky it can be? That's why it is so important to keep a pure mind and burn off all of those old imprints and contamination.

The good news is that if you keep sincerely focused on and working toward the true and ultimate original God, nothing less, all those other "gods" and spiritual beings must help you or let you pass.

That's why we always work toward true sincerity. We reach our utmost sincerity and align ourselves with it. Then as we grow stronger and purer, we work toward even more sincerity, and once again align ourselves with that higher sincerity. Sincere and align, sincere and align, over and over. This is our practice toward Tao.

In the meantime, it helps to have a master to guide you on this journey. When you take off in a jet plane, you often must pass through layers of clouds before you rise above them into pure and clear sky. The same is true in our spiritual journey. Before we can reach the clear and pure kingdom of God, we have many cloudy and confusing layers we must penetrate. A master can give you help in how to navigate through this cloud layer until you can see clearly for yourself.

Stay Connected – Do Not Rely on Your Own Power

If you connect to that ultimate God, it's like you are plugged into the outlet in the wall. Those other spiritual energies cannot touch you because the voltage is too high. We have to go high enough to touch that Net, then that nonsense thinking in our brain dissolves, and every evil, all those small gods, cannot touch you. That voltage is too high. They have to step away and let you go.

But if you try to rely on your own energy, your voltage is not high enough to offer such protection. When you rely on your own energy, you will simply drain your battery. This is the mistake some people make when working with Chi for healing, martial arts or spiritual readings. They rely on their own power.

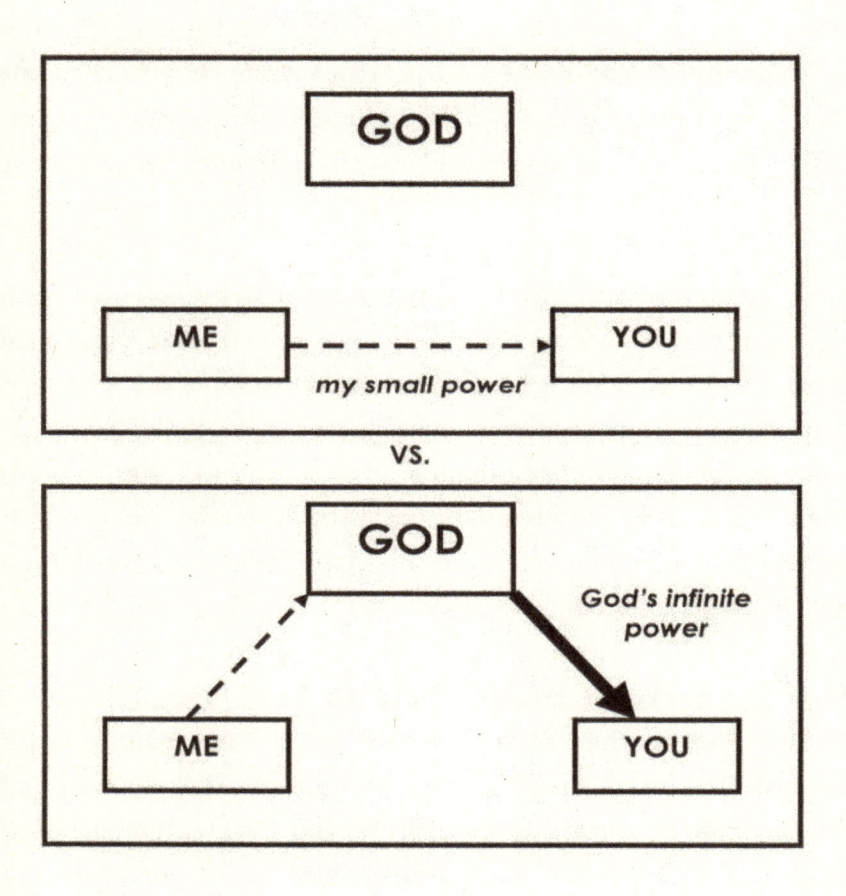

```
┌─────────────────────────────────────┐
│              ┌───────┐              │
│              │  GOD  │              │
│              └───────┘              │
│                                     │
│  ┌──────┐                 ┌──────┐  │
│  │  ME  │----------→      │ YOU  │  │
│  └──────┘  my small power └──────┘  │
└─────────────────────────────────────┘
                 VS.
┌─────────────────────────────────────┐
│              ┌───────┐              │
│              │  GOD  │              │
│              └───────┘              │
│                       God's infinite│
│                           power     │
│                              ↓      │
│  ┌──────┐                 ┌──────┐  │
│  │  ME  │                 │ YOU  │  │
│  └──────┘                 └──────┘  │
└─────────────────────────────────────┘
```

If you come to me and you are sick, and I connect directly to you using my own power to help you, my voltage is so low it cannot accomplish very much. I'm trying to help you from the power in my little battery. But if, when you come to me, I go to the true

God first and connect and let God be the one to help you, it's as if I plug into the wall outlet. Then, it's that unlimited power of God that goes to you. That power is much stronger than my little battery.

We have to continually connect to God to charge our life energy. That's why it's important to learn how to connect.

But sometimes we fool ourselves into thinking we are plugged in when we aren't. We think we are using God's energy, when we are really draining our own. Under this mistaken notion, we keep using our power until we are dangerously low, without even being aware of it.

If we unplug our cell phone and walk far away from the charger, it still works just fine. We can still use it. It still lights up and beeps. It works exactly the same way as if it were still plugged into the wall. We have the illusion that our cell phone is perfectly okay and will keep going forever. But in reality, as long as we are disconnected from that charger, at some point in time it's going to run out of power. Furthermore, it will probably run out of power when we are out on a dark road with a flat tire.

Likewise, our own Chi can give us the illusion that we have a lot of power and are humming along just fine. But in a critical moment, you could find that your life energy is no longer strong enough to sustain or protect you. So after we charge up, we should be very grateful and not stray too far away from that outlet where we can charge up again. We should always remember to go back and connect with that true God.

We have to get that real ability just like Jesus had. When Jesus meditated, he connected to God. One woman truly believed that if she could just touch him she would be healed. So that's what she did. She touched the hem of Jesus' robe with sincere faith and was completely healed. The moment she touched him with that true sincerity, Jesus felt that power go through his energy and asked: "Who touched me?" He knew he was connected to God, plugged into that outlet, and he felt that surge go through him and out to that woman. He didn't claim it was his power that healed her. He told her that it was her faith that brought that healing. Her faith and sincerity touched him while he was connected to that Net, and this triggered that power to flow from God through him.

If we try to use our own power to heal and help others, we're not only relying on our own small battery, we are also relying on our own little human mind. We think we are smart enough to decide who needs help, and how they should be helped. If you look around you will find that when people pray they often tell God what to do. We have no such wisdom like God's wisdom. We cannot see enough or think clearly enough to know what a certain person really needs. We cannot use spiritual power in a pure and true way like God can.

When we try to use our own spiritual power and our own little minds, we are like the old couple in that fairy tale. The old man catches a fish in the river, but doesn't realize it is a magical fish. He brings the fish home for his wife to cook. But when the fish sees the old woman and her frying pan, the fish says, "Stop! If you let me go back into the river, I will grant you three magical wishes. You just say the word and whatever you want will magically appear."

Well the old couple never heard a fish talk before, and they were very amazed. The wife said, "If that fish can talk, then he must have very great magic. Let's let him go and keep the three magic wishes." So the old man took the fish back to the river bank and let it go.

When the old man returned to the cottage, he said, "I am so hungry! I wish I had a sausage." Suddenly, a huge and delicious sausage magically appeared on a plate in front of him. He started eating it with great pleasure.

"You idiot!" cried his wife. "You just wasted one of our three magic wishes on a sausage. You should have wished for gold or riches. You are so stupid. I wish that sausage was your nose!" At those words, suddenly the sausage disappeared. Instead, it now grew out of the old man's face, exactly where his nose had been. The couple both gasped, but then wept bitterly when they realized they had now used up two magic wishes. Of course, you know the ending. The couple had to use the third wish to restore the old man's real nose.

We don't even know how and when to use this power in the right way because our mind is so limited and our judgment is impure. By connecting to God and allowing God to do the job, the benefit is that God sees and knows everything, and knows exactly what to do and when and how to do it.

When you have the power to heal with your Chi, or to use energy for spiritual reading to see the future or past, or to use energy in other ways that help people, when you see somebody suffering, it's very tempting to interfere. But without God's insight, you don't know whether this suffering may be necessary, or if, by your effort to help, you are interfering with God's plan in some way and its better to leave things alone.

If you automatically reach out and help with your own energy, you are only connecting to yourself and your own judgment. Your Chi healing will burn up a lot of your own energy and might not even work to help the other person in the long run. The other person's problem might come right back in a day or two, because it is based on a spiritual debt or difficulty that you cannot even see, much less resolve.

Also, when you play God, thinking you know the right solution for somebody else's problem on your own, you may actually be blocking others from the opportunity to access the real God. They start to rely on you and other "healers" rather than working to clean up their lives and connect to God for themselves.

If I want to connect directly with you to help you with *my* energy, that means I have to pull my plug out from the wall and disconnect from God first before I can connect to you. By doing this, I automatically lose access to that highest power.

Instead of me letting go of God in order to connect with you, I'd rather reach out to connect to God and let God be the one to connect to you. Then you benefit from the power and wisdom of God, and any solution will be the right solution.

Disconnecting from God and trying to operate like God on our own power is what made this world so mixed-up to begin with and why nothing works out in the end. Why bring this same approach to your spiritual and healing work?

Remember, the real God is a power, a super-mind, an ultimate force that's beyond our comprehension. This Creator simply thinks "Let there be sausage," and a wonderful sausage appears.

In our world, we like to mimic that power and give ourselves the illusion that we are like God and have God's power. In our case, we raise money at our job so that we can go to a restaurant, which pays a delivery truck that then pays for a butcher who buys a pig and kills it and mashes it up into sausage. All of this is done so that when I walk in and sit down in this restaurant, I can say, "I want sausage." A waitress brings a steaming hot sausage on a plate and sets it in front of me. Voila! Our elaborate fake system gives me the illusion that I am like God, and that I can materialize a sausage.

Those false man-made systems whisper in our ear: "Why do you need God? You don't need God. If you get sick, just go to my hospital. If you need food, come to my grocery store. If you get lonely, turn on the television. If we have any problem on our planet, don't worry! Our technology will fix everything. Wait until you die, then you can go to God." We are lulled into a false security by all the man-made creations around us. We lose that urgency to go back and connect.

In mundane day-to-day affairs, it's okay to go along on our own judgment and power. If I hire you to come and repair my roof, but you don't repair my roof the right way and it still leaks, I'll pick up the phone to call you so that we can talk about it. But if you come to me with a matter of life or death, an issue of healing or suffering, I know that this is God's matter for sure. I wouldn't try to deal with it on my own. I go to God. If this is God's matter, I go to God.

People complain to me, "Master, if we have the power to help people with our Chi, but we don't, won't they think we are uncaring and selfish? What if we go to God and God will not let us help somebody else, won't they think we or God are unkind?"

The answer is that when you connect with God, you don't care what anyone thinks. Whenever I stop and think about what somebody else is doing, thinking, or what they are going to say, I stop looking to God.

Your connection to God will give you enlightenment about what's going on so that you can see things clearly. Connecting to God and knowing the truth is more important than trying to change the situation, and much more important that what the other person thinks.

To know the truth, the first thing you have to do is know nothing. Erase everything you've learned. In our mind, we can often see many different solutions, many different possibilities, and many ways to help. So we use our judgment to choose from our many ideas. If we see "many" that's an illusion. Lao Tzu says, *"Embrace the One Power."*

Remember, oftentimes in this world we actually are dealing with a dark force. But why should I fight with evil with my own small power? I just go to God and then God will fight with evil. But if you don't upgrade yourself to contact God, and try to go out and change this world, or help others with their suffering with your own energy and your own contaminated judgment, that's risky business. Then you are like a rabbit or lamb being lured into the slaughterhouse by evil. Don't fight with the tiger's claw, don't fight with the rhinoceros' horn, go to God.

When you connect with God, you have that protection wherever you go. In the old days, everyone was afraid somebody else would call them a "witch" behind their back. In most cases, if enough people thought you were a witch, it meant you were going to get killed. If I say, "Sally is a witch," and gossip spreads, pretty soon everybody thinks Sally is a witch. It doesn't matter what Sally thinks, or whether Sally really is a witch or not, she's going to get killed.

But if Sally holds onto that One Power, the people around her won't even be able to formulate the thought in their mind that "Sally is a witch." Their mind cannot even create the idea. They cannot think evil about Sally no matter how hard they try. They start to think, "Sally is a *whubba, blah, werble*...... Look at those beautiful apples for sale. I think I'll go buy some!" That's why you just hold onto that One Power instead of defending yourself or seeking to protect yourself from others.

If evil attacks me, that means I haven't gone to God yet, or am incapable of going to God, or have weakened or lost my connection to God. It means I better do everything possible to go back and reconnect with God.

If the majority of people in this world were to wake up and go to God, evil would become very weak. Taichi and moving meditation allow us to clean up and qualify ourselves to make that connection to God. But before we clean ourselves up, we are greatly distracted by evil.

The Five Senses Can Trick You
In our human world, we learn and "know" and judge things as true or false, good or bad, based on the information we receive from our five senses. There is nothing wrong with our five senses. However, our five senses are not the highest level of truth. They are a lower level and can often give us wrong information.

Why are our five senses a lower level of truth? All sensory perception is made possible by that piece of God inside us. However, sensory perception is a downgraded form of energy from the origin. After all, the original energy has no color, no sound, no smell and no flavor. That's why any time we see, hear, smell, taste or touch something, we are never connecting to the highest true original energy, only a downgraded version of it.

That's why many old teachings refer to this world as an "illusion." It's because we are relying on our five senses which give us only partial and sometimes false information. Lao Tzu says:

> *"The five colors blind your eyes.*
> *The five sounds deafen your ears.*
> *The five flavors ruin your taste.*
> *Too much hunting and games*
> *confuse your mind."*
>
> Lao Tzu, *Tao Te Ching*, Chapter 12

Whenever you believe the evidence of your five senses without connecting with God for the truth, you become blind, deaf and dumb. We have to transform ourselves so that we can access information from the original energy, which is higher and purer than our five senses. That way we can rise above this "illusion" so that we can know the truth. Once you can connect with original life energy, you will be transformed in such a way that you can then see true things, hear true things, smell true things, taste true things and feel only true things.

That's why, in our Tao Gong moving meditation, we meditate on a point in our Dan Tian, the center of the lower stomach area behind your navel. While we meditate, we pull in our sense of sight and try and look inside toward that Dan Tian. We try and see what is there. We use our hearing and try to hear that point, that Dan Tian. Is there any sound? We use our sense of smell and direct it to our lower stomach area and ask, "Can I smell anything?" We imagine the root of our tongue extending down to that point, and we ask ourselves, can I taste anything?

We try and concentrate the power of all of our senses and bring them back to the source point of our original life energy. That Dan Tian is where your life began. It's the point at which you were connected to your mother in the womb. It is where you meditate to try to reawaken the memory of that first single cell.

After all, where did our sense of sight, hearing, taste, smell and feeling come from originally? They all came from that first single cell. Your nose, your ears, your eyes, your skin cells, all developed from that first root cell. That single cell carried the power to create and fuel all of your senses. You want to go backward and bring all those powers back to their origin. You want to become like that original stem cell, one undifferentiated powerful source of energy, connected to the origin. Cells divided into five zones of taste buds, and cells that specialized into rods and cones taking in light and the five colors are already downgraded from the full potential of that first single cell. They are no longer stem cells.

In the book *"Nine Nights with the Taoist Master,"* I include a diagram to help readers understand the various levels of sense and perception and which senses are closer or further to that signal of original energy inside of us. On the next page is a smaller version of that diagram to show how our thinking and senses relate to that piece of Te inside of us.

You'll see in this diagram that the outermost ring represents our thinking. The thinking mind, because it is so complicated and stretched so far away from that Te, is our least reliable source of information. The reason our mind is the least reliable is because our mind can be influenced by so many outside signals, by so many variables. It can often mislead us.

The next ring is our sense of sight. It is the second *least* reliable source of information. It's less reliable than the other senses, precisely because it is so tightly connected to our mind. You are constantly and instantly interpreting and reacting to everything you see with your mind. When ten different witnesses with perfectly good pairs of eyes see the same car accident, you will often get ten different reports of what happened. That's because the same sights were filtered through ten different minds.

Ironically, many people consider sight their best source of truth. There's even a saying, "I have to see it to believe it!" But it is very easy to create visual illusions in our world. We have paintings, movies, mirrors, colored lights and television. All these flashing lights, colors and reflections cause us to see things that are not

232   TAO: THE WAY OF GOD

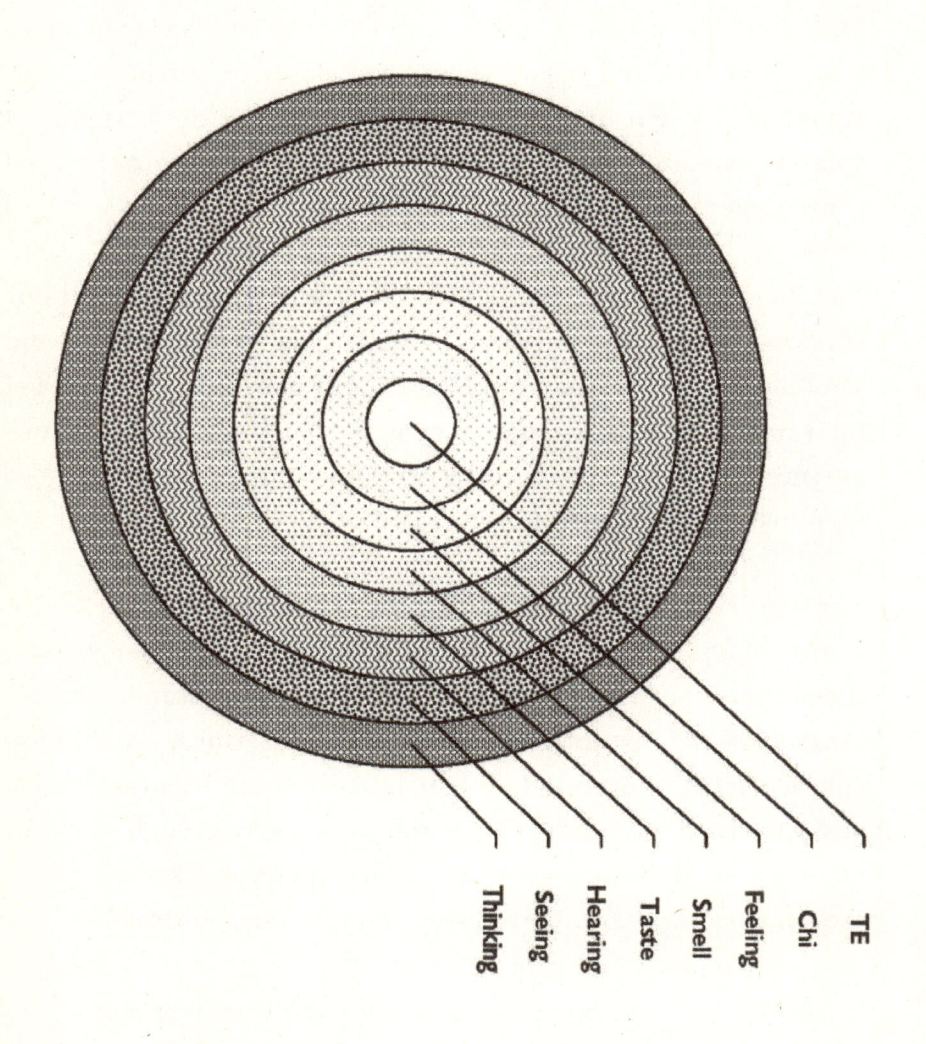

- TE
- Chi
- Feeling
- Smell
- Taste
- Hearing
- Seeing
- Thinking

actually there. That's how most magicians create their stunning array of tricks. They learn that it's very easy to fool the eyes.

Even when you see a simple color, you have a subconscious judgment. Colors can deceive you. What color is the origin?

Light, color and images can be deceiving. Surely you have heard spiritual people claim "God is Light!" But God and the truth of God is much greater and far superior than light. After all, in the beginning God said "Let there be Light!" God came first.

This is why I tell my students that if they see light, color or images while they are meditating that they shouldn't stop and shouldn't interpret them. I tell them to keep going.

Our sense of hearing is a little more reliable than our eyesight, but not much. Why? Because our hearing is still is connected very tightly to our thoughts and interpretations. Our ears can be easily tricked too.

Our senses of taste and smell are more reliable, because they are more primary and less subject to thoughts and interpretations. But they are still far from perfect. Modern chemistry is capable of creating many artificial fragrances and flavors that fool our nose and our tongue. These fake smells and flavors trick us into eating very unhealthy foods that can even harm us.

Our sense of feeling is the most reliable of our five human senses. What we feel is very direct. It has a better chance of actually bypassing our mind, thoughts and interpretations. It is more primal, more foundational than hearing and seeing.

Since our sense of feeling is less complicated, more basic and reliable, it is actually closer to the true feeling of life energy. That's why we can use that sense of feeling in our meditation to restore our true feeling of the life energy inside of us. That true feeling of life energy in turn rests on top of the Te.

Now you understand why we stress using "feeling" so much in our moving meditation. It's also why we try to keep our mind and senses in a state of stillness, we want to be able to be so still and focused that we can feel everything going on while we practice. Eventually, we want to be able to feel our whole body at the same time. We want to restore our lost ability to feel things that we forgot how to feel.

I often ask my students during Taichi practice, "Can you feel your ear? Can you feel your kidney? Can you use your ear to turn, along with your whole body?" We've lost our ability to feel ourselves. If you try right now, can you feel your pancreas? I bet you cannot. I'll bet the vast majority of people have lost the ability to feel virtually all of their internal organs. It's not that your pancreas has no nerve cells and it's impossible to feel it. When you are sick and diseased, then you can feel your organs. Your pancreas can really hurt when it's infected!

But if you cannot feel your own pancreas, your own ear, or your own liver at will, how can you learn to feel and use your life energy? How can you claim to feel what's going on in the patient you are trying to heal? How can you feel and mange your opponent's energy in martial arts? More importantly, how can you learn to feel that subtle Te inside of you?

Our senses are made possible by Chi and the intelligence of that original energy inside of us. But they, like everything else, have separated from their original connection to that pure power of God. If we had that original connection, we wouldn't need our eyes, our skin, our ears, nose, or mouth.

There was an interesting study done recently by scientists on what really happens when we communicate with each other. Scientists monitored a number of subjects' brain waves while they said basic words like "apple," "dog," or "cat." They mapped which parts of the brain fired when a Chinese or German speaker saw a picture of an apple and then said "apple." Do you know what they discovered? They found out that the same exact part of the brain fired when each different subject said "apple" and the same part fired when they said "dog" no matter what language they spoke. French, Chinese, or German, the same part of each person's brain governed the word for apple, while another similar part governed the word for dog.

What does this research show us? There's a brain location, wave or signal for "apple" that we each have inside of us that doesn't involve language at all. It's the same for everybody, no matter where they are raised. This higher level or original idea of apple goes above our language and above what we can speak and hear.

If we can go to this higher place, and find out how we can use this original framework to communicate, we can communicate without words.

There are people who are somehow able to pick up these signals or waves. There's a story of an old Taoist who could communicate with nature. This Taoist understood birds when they chirped to each other. He could hear that they actually talked to each other and exchanged all sorts of information. One day, right after a brief summer storm, he heard birds talking about how they just saw a tiger attack and kill a deer. But the birds reported to each other that this thunderstorm had scared the tiger away before he could eat the deer. This left the freshly killed deer still warm and laying in the field. So the monk quickly went to the village nearby and told them to hurry over to the next field, because they would find a deer that had just been killed by a tiger. If they took pitchforks to keep away the tiger, they could keep the meat for themselves.

From time to time in our world, there are people who have strange abilities like that old Taoist. Some people hear sounds with their eyes. They actually see the vibration of the sound as a pattern or a color. Some people can taste music or hear colors. If a Taoist meditates very dedicatedly to bring everything down to stillness, they touch the source of all awareness and can pick up information beyond what people ordinarily taste, smell, feel, see and hear.

In the old days, the Chinese healers diagnosed your health problem by listening to the sound of your voice, evaluating your smell, looking at the color of your skin and tongue and fingernails, feeling your various pulses. But the highest level healers weren't just gathering sense information and making mental diagnoses based on what they learned in medical class. The highest level healers were using their deep awareness to detect higher energy signals that gave them the truth about your condition, your energy imbalance, and even the spiritual source of your health problem.

These stories are a testimony to the fact that our over-reliance on the five senses limits our true potential. If we don't empty our reliance on those outer senses, we won't be able to hear or feel the true perception from our life energy. None of that outside information from our five senses can help us detect that Net, and they can even prevent us from detecting it.

That's why we want to bring all these senses back to the Dan Tian. It's okay to have color, tone, or different flavors, but do not forget to go back to their root – the Te.

Our Fakeness can be Used to Mislead Us

Your senses can be used to mislead, control and manipulate you. For example, Nazi Germany employed many tactics strategically for ruling and dominating people. They designed rituals, uniforms, hats, tones of color, all meant to send out a message that would make people submit.

Many customs in today's scientific world, our medical world, our business world are copied from Nazi Germany. For example, in Nazi Germany the top officers' hats were much higher than the hats of lower ranking officers. (The Nazi's actually copied that from Catholic bishops.) Today you can see our commercial airlines copying this with their airplane pilots' hats. For awhile, this was also copied in the field of nursing. A higher hat gives out that signal that the one who wears it has higher authority.

In America, our leaders started using Nazi tricks after World War II. Prior to World War II, presidents stood out on a podium or at the back of a train when they spoke to people. They might be driven in a car from here to there with little fanfare. But after World War II, whenever the president came out in public, he had a motorcade. They learned that from Hitler and his motorcades.

There's a famous incident when Hitler landed in an airfield and came out of the back of the airplane waving. A young girl ran to him to give him a flower. It gave a subconscious idea of a supernatural leader coming down from the sky to save the day. After that incident, American presidents liked to mimic that idea. They would come down from the sky in their airplane to be greeted by big brass bands as the walked out of the plane waving to the people. They would hold babies and have their pictures taken with children to look like good fathers, people we can trust.

No person should be tricked into giving away their trust to anybody else but God. But why do humans give that up? We give up our trust to those who are unworthy because of the sin, flaws, defects and fake ideas inside of us. We listen to that imagery and manipulation that tries to control us, and we follow it because we are trained to like it.

When somebody tries to act, talk, claim, and dress-up like a king or some power over us, and they claim to be higher than anyone else, that is evil. It's the devil's act. Such manipulation is anti-Tao. Anybody who tries to win your trust away from God and only God is anti-God.

How many influences outside of God's net can affect us? How many influences outside of God's net are we exposed to every day? A lot! Language, gravity, light, tone of voice, they all distort that original signal. That's why our efforts to learn from and communicate with each other often fail.

If you and I talk using language, there's always a problem. Even if we speak the same language, my tone of voice, or your perception of my tone or intention, can alter the message. It's easy for us to have blockage when we try to communicate. If I say, "Martha, you are very *nice*???" and I have a tone of doubt in my voice, this can mean I don't think Martha is very nice at all. If I say "Martha, you are <u>very</u> nice!" that could mean I find Martha attractive. I can also say very firmly, "Martha, <u>you</u> are very nice." That could mean I heartily approve of something Martha just did.

In all three occasions, I've said exactly the same words. But what I mean is totally different. What Martha hears and how Martha interprets these tones and words can add any number of distortions. Perhaps Martha had a bad day. Maybe she doesn't like me. Maybe she can't hear too well out of her left ear and misses a word or two. I don't know!

So our language, our environment, our thoughts, and many other factors give us distortion when we communicate outside of that Net. This ultimate Net is clear, fine, weak, and almost non-existent. It is emptiness with no smell, no vibration, no color, and no tone. When I connect to that Net and communicate to you through that network, then I can send a true message to you that's not distorted. I don't need language, sound, tone or the written word.

But if we talk out here away from that Net, it's all fake, not true, and distorted. What's the answer to the age-old question, "Why can't everyone just get along?" We can't because we keep trying to communicate and get along with each other outside of that Net where everything we say and do is distorted.

The distortion of truth is our biggest challenge in trying to teach and learn about Tao. That's why Lao Tzu says: "*The Tao that can be spoken of is not the true Tao.*" Any time we speak of it in words, we are speaking in the dimension of distortion. The most difficult obstacle we have in reaching Tao is fakeness, lies and everything that's "not truth." That's why Lao Tzu says:

> "*Those who really know do not talk.*
> *Those who talk do not know the truth.*"
> Lao Tzu, *Tao Te Ching*, Chapter 55

Look how pitiful we are if we have to go through speech. When we speak we have so much distortion. That's why Lao Tzu doesn't want to speak about Tao because when you use language you automatically have to use something that is fake!

To connect to God is both very easy and very challenging. The challenge is to get rid of the distortion, the "less-than-God" stuff that blocks us. The easy part is that if we can go back to that piece of God in us, it will drill a hole right through all of that inner and outer contamination and connect right back to Tao. It's like a tunnel or a worm hole that bypasses all that distortion.

Through that piece of God inside of us, we share that Net with whatever is 15 billion light years away. If I vibrate here, that Net picks it up over there right away. It's instantaneous. This is because we are not using lesser media like the speed of light. Electrons and radio waves are still particle-like material that takes time to travel from broadcaster to receiver. Even those energies are subject to distortion. We are going far beyond even that sort of communication when we touch that Net.

In our limited world, we are bound by physical material. Our body is material; therefore all of our senses are based on a material world. The reason my senses and this material world impress me a lot is because I'm trapped in here, so I don't think beyond this. And because I can't think beyond this, I stay trapped. This is a disaster, because it prevents us from connecting back to God. I worship this low-level material stuff and my senses instead, even though those senses give us wrong information.

If you are in a jail, it restricts you. But let's say you like and worship that jail cell because you've been in it for so long. You no longer consider anything outside of that jail. Because you like and worship it, and don't believe there is anything outside, you will never get out. Only those who know there is something better outside of jail can even hope to get out.

Likewise, we too easily get trapped in simple understandings that make sense to us, so we are never willing to think further than these. We never bother to figure out how we can get beyond our own logic or our own five senses. We make our own jail out of our limited thinking. We are trapped.

How can we get out of our thinking traps? We must move towards Te first. We use moving meditation to strip and burn our thinking, burn our imagination, burn our mind activity, and burn our allegiance to our five senses. We reduce all that until we find the Te.

Many self-development groups like to emphasize teachings that use even more thinking, use mind power, or use mental visualization and imagination. They are very popular because that approach is easy to sell. It's our natural inclination to go that way, to want to rely on our own mind and power. It is very hard to go the other way, away from thinking and towards the Te.

To go backwards to Te you need to have no purpose while you follow that original and natural pathway back to where your life began. There's a precise method and there are no shortcuts. Our cells split in a logical and orderly way. Our body forms itself in a logical sequential way, building each section in order. When you use moving meditation to go back to Te, you have to go backward that same logical way. You have to follow the same sequential process in reverse. If you don't follow the same process, the mind may condense and try to move down to the Dan Tian, but it may not hit that Te directly. It will bounce off or vibrate out on the perimeter. But by following the ancient training preserved in real authentic Taichi and Tao Gong meditation, you can learn from a Master how to do this sequential meditation properly.

Free Will Means Freedom from Evil

What is evil? Evil is anything "not original," "not genuine." Evil is any attempt to misinterpret or misrepresent God's original intentions. God's power will bring you back toward the Origin, while evil's power will interfere with such an effort.

Human beings stepped down from the dimension of God (like the story of when Adam and Eve were chased out of the Garden) because they "woke-up" and got their own ideas. As soon as you get your own idea, you get chased out of that ultimate dimension. As soon as you are a different frequency from the frequency of God, you get squeezed out of that highest dimension. That's why the more you are educated, the more of your own ideas you have, the further away you are from that original frequency.

Whenever I say that we separate ourselves from God when we have our own ideas, one question always comes up. Students ask me, "Master, do we have free will? If we are not supposed to have our own ideas, doesn't that mean God doesn't want us to be free? Are we supposed to be just robots or puppets?"

People have been arguing about the question of free will versus predestination for centuries. People wonder whether everything we do is already decided by God or whether we have choices. They wonder why we were given free will if we are only supposed to surrender it to God's will. Many religious scholars and philosophers like to debate about free will versus predestination and God's will too. They usually give up and call the issue a paradox. The reason it is such a paradox for them is that they approach this topic from a limited human perspective.

Our idea of freedom in this world is an illusion. We think we are making decisions and charting our own course based on our own free will. But many times the things we like, the choices we make, the consequences we suffer, are affected by the contaminated energy and its past history that coats us.

If you have energy that was once used by a banker, chances are that the world of finance will make sense and appeal to you. So when you choose a career in banking, you believe you did this out of your own free will. But did you really?

If you carry recycled energy used by a person in the past who suffered a violent and traumatic death, you may struggle with fear and depression and not know why. You may reach out to drugs, alcohol or even suicide for relief. Did you freely make those bad choices, or were you propelled by the damage leftover from the recycled energy within your Chi?

You meet and fall in love with somebody, but what you don't know is that the two of you each carries recycled energy used by two others who were enemies at one time. You marry each other and wind up miserable. You are always fighting and end up divorced. You wonder why the two of you could never get along despite your love for each other and all the counseling and self-help books you sought answers from.

In all of these cases you thought you had free will, but you were affected by the pollution that steered your preferences, experiences and choices. Because you never saw, felt or understood that spiritual dimension and the truth about your recycled Chi, your feeling of freedom was just an illusion. In a way, by unconsciously responding to these old negative signals, you were more like a robot or a puppet rather than a truly free person.

These old signals trapped in our energy are why it can feel like our lives are outside of our control — especially when we make the same personal mistakes over and over again. We can blame the stars, God, or some quirk of fate that makes us pick the wrong friends again and again — friends who end up hurting us. What we don't see or understand is that we carry the energy of an old army soldier who killed all these people in a battlefield long ago. Their energy seeks you out for revenge and finds you. The energy of those you killed is now being used by people in your circle of "friends." Both you and your so-called friends are unaware that this dynamic is going on, so you play out what you think are current events in your lives, but always end up at odds with each other based on that old history.

So does that mean that by these old signals we are predestined by God or karma? Well it is more like we are predestined to play out the mistakes of our polluted energy, and continue down the dead-end road of being separated from God until we make a decision to change. You can change your course. To do that, you have to go back to God. The truth is that God is free will. You never find true freedom until you reconnect with God.

We lock ourselves into such a limited dimension, a one-way dead end street. But if you touch God, then you have free will and understand what freedom really means. Your human level free will won't get you anywhere or change anything. It's simply not powerful enough. But if you contact that Net, then you have the ability to rise above the limitations of this world and see the truth about the people, situations and choices in your life.

Escape From Wrong Thinking

As long as we remain in our human level, we are in false truth. We believe what we see and experience around us is true, but it's not real. It's not real because it's incomplete. It's partial truth. Our world is like a fictional bubble world. We think it's real, because we cannot see the rest of what is going on outside of our little bubble.

But if we are in the spiritual Net, we are in the original force building this entire known universe — including our life, our thinking and our mind. We came from there. It's the origin. When we go back there, we are no longer subject to this limited dead end approach. We are outside that bubble.

It takes a big effort to swim backward toward our origin. We have to get rid of and purify a lot of stuff to qualify ourselves. It's hard work to worship the real God. Our way back to God is like an epic journey. On that journey we are fighting the devil, turning away from evil, resisting temptation, and become willing to give up many things.

The hardest part of our journey is that all of our views of God are based on fake analogies and wrong thinking that we've accumulated, so we tend to end up following the wrong map.

We are conditioned by evil toward so many wrong ways of thinking. The idea of ownership, for example, is the worst form of fakeness. Who ever thought we could own the land on the face of this Earth that we all share? What a crazy idea. Even now, when you purchase a piece of land, you don't really own it. If you don't pay taxes on that land to the government, they can take it away. You don't even own your own body, or your own Chi or your own Te. What makes you think you can own land or anything else?

Wrong thinking drives us outward for our answers instead of inward toward our Te. When we are bored we go outside looking for some action. When we have problems, we go outside to create solutions. We see everybody else doing and experiencing so many things *out there*, so we figure we better go out there too and try them. Guess what? Whenever you aim outward to look for answers in this fictional bubble world, you just lost your Center.

When you have the Way, you stay right there. If for any reason you get pushed out of that connection with God, you work to realign yourself with that Center again. Doing this is what we call practicing *"Tao Shau Lian"*— align and practice, align and practice, over and over and over. Align with what? The Tao.

If you receive wrong information, or believe outside sources and align with the wrong map on your journey, that's tough luck for you. You will end up practicing for years and wind up never reaching Tao. That's why so few people reach Tao. We keep aligning ourselves with garbage and distortions of the truth.

That's why we have to go through days, months, years, even decades of training. The impact of our history and the world around us trains us to read the wrong map, or interpret the correct map in the wrong way. We have to unlearn the wrong information, and constantly correct ourselves. We must dedicate ourselves to moving meditation, and constantly expose ourselves to the correct teaching of this wisdom. Then our map straightens out and we start making progress.

Pay attention the next time you drive your car down a straight and narrow highway. You'll notice that your hands on the wheel are constantly correcting, constantly adjusting for little bumps, winds, and small deviations. Sure it appears that you are driving in a straight line, but it takes constant adjustment to keep going straight.

Many people reading the many words in this book will interpret them in their own way, depending on how they've been educated or the society they live in. The teachings in this book will be heard differently by each person depending on the mental blockages or energy pollution of whoever reads it.

I have had people study my work over the years who are very violent at heart. They look to my words to find some excuse to go out and use power and force to hurt people. They will pick up bits and parts of what I say and say to themselves, "Master Liao says it's okay to go and hurt other people." I've seen students from all walks of life take these teachings and fit them to their own interpretations, or use bits and pieces of them to justify a wide variety of different beliefs and lifestyles.

The energies behind wrong interpretations have a history and a mission too. They come here to pollute and lead people down the wrong track. Many real and true spiritual teachings have been hijacked and altered beyond all recognition over the years. You can find examples of this within many major religions.

These wrong interpretations don't just apply to religion, but to any and all areas of our lives. After all, every fake idea is ultimately a religion when we believe and worship it: our monetary system, college degrees, our social customs, etc.

It doesn't matter how hard you work, weep, pray or try to control the world around you, bad people can take over and spit out a wrong interpretation of anything. They want to separate you from the oneness of God, and bring back the many layers of god.

It's hard to know where wrong thinking and evil will arise. It's not always immediately obvious. At one point a nice little baby came into this world, so cute sitting on the floor and playing with his toys. His name was little Adolf Hitler. When he was a young man he went to school, even became an artist. He was a conscientious and sensitive young man, interested in health and spirituality. As he got older, he looked around his country and saw unfairness and suffering and wanted to fix it. He spoke to others about his ideas, and soon many thousands of people saw him as a crusader for the salvation of his people. Look what this apparently innocent past led to. Initially you wouldn't be able to tell he would become the evil he ultimately personified. You couldn't tell what wrong thinking went on in his head so that he could later justify the sort of brutality that led to the slaughter of over 6 million people.

Everyone feels they are right and are doing what is necessary and good. They have an excuse or explanation for why they act and think the way that they do. Even criminals in jail who have done terrible things, often feel inside that they were justified and doing what was necessary and good at the time of their crime. They almost never think that they were at fault. The people at the helm of corrupt finance, government, war, industrial pollution, education and business all feel at some level that they are doing what is just and good. This is one reason why no matter how much you guard against it, evil can slip in and take control of any artificial system.

That's why I tell my students "never graduate." Never feel that you have arrived and are immune from being misled. Be vigilant against wrong thinking. Constantly practice, constantly work to readjust and align yourself with that true feeling, and keep working to be clean, humble and going toward the one true God.

Acceptance, Forgiveness and Ignoring Evil

If everybody ignores wrong doing, ignores hurt and forgives others for causing their suffering, this bad energy has no more fuel. It disappears. But we cannot seem to ignore evil. Instead, we react and set even more evil in motion.

Wars in many regions of our world keep happening over and over because one group is out for revenge against another and kill them in return for all those killed in the previous war. But then the families of those they kill today come back for more revenge tomorrow, and the cycle continues forever.

The old teachings of Tao stressed *"no self and no enemy."* This principle was taught so that disciples could learn to ignore evil and not hold such thoughts in their mind. If evil energy wants to attack you and you don't respond, or if you deny the recognition that it's evil, it's as if there is no energy to sustain the conflict. After all, there must be two opponents to have a fight. If you don't protect yourself, and instead you ignore it and go do something else, that tiger has no place to put his claw. If you don't respond to an intention to hurt you, then you have no enemy.

On the other hand, if someone wants to attack you and you immediately react to protect yourself, you automatically have an enemy.

You don't have to be attacked physically to have an enemy. Situations in your life can become your enemy if you let them. For example, it is part of our human condition to suffer. But when we resist and fight and work so hard to stop our own suffering, we give it more power and make it our enemy.

That's why it's important to be patient and gentle, stay calm and move forward slowly if you are suffering. If there is a nail sticking out of a board and that irritates you, it does no good to smack your hand down on top of that nail. The idea is not to punch and kick and try to get out of your suffering. Find a way to accept, forgive and move forward calmly.

The Amish people provided a very good example of handling great suffering gently and accepting it with forgiveness. Many Americans will remember the headlines a few years ago about a shooter who came to an Amish community and killed many young children in their little schoolhouse. The Amish people did not try to get even, they did not go on the media raging for justice. No. They quietly, with no fanfare, buried each of the small children in a simple ceremony. When interviewed later, we saw an amazing story of the triumph of forgiveness. The spokespeople for the community said that they all realized that the man who killed these children was very disturbed and injured in his soul. They forgave him.

Not only that, when money poured in from around the country, they shared an equal portion among each of the victim's families, including an equal portion to the widow of the shooter. They realized she was a victim too, since she lost a husband to this evil.

They realized it was better to forgive than to rage and fight and allow that evil to survive inside their heads and hearts. They knew that if they held onto that hate, that sorrow, that blame, then they would automatically cut themselves off from God. By forgiveness, they could keep that line of connection open.

But even though forgiveness is a very effective tool that can be used by spiritual people to raise their energy, believe it or not, it still isn't a sign of somebody at the highest level. If you are at the highest level, you transcend the need for forgiveness altogether. Why? Because you see nothing as evil and nobody can hurt you, so there is nothing to forgive.

There was an old story about a young village girl who was about fourteen years old. Like many young girls, she had a boyfriend who lived nearby. She would sneak out to see him when her parents were busy with their farm work. This young girl accidentally got pregnant by her boyfriend. She didn't want him to get in trouble, so she lied to her family and told them that she got pregnant by the monk who lived in the little local temple.

The family was so outraged that they told all their neighbors. All the villagers organized and charged down to the temple and berated the monk: "You are supposed to be so holy. You liar! You fake! You are a dirty and evil man! Shame on you. We will no longer donate to your temple. When that baby comes, you will take the baby and raise it yourself. Why should we raise your child?"

The monk looked down and said, "Okay." True to their word, when the baby was born, the villagers dropped it in a basket at the temple door. The monk opened the door and silently brought the baby inside.

The monk quietly raised the baby and never said anything. Over the years, the baby grew to be a handsome young boy and was very intelligent. That young village girl eventually married her boyfriend when she got older. Now older and wiser and with a good husband who was the baby's true father, she felt sorry and really wanted to get that boy back. She mustered all of her courage and told the truth to the whole village, that the child they gave the monk so long ago was really her husband's child.

The village felt bad and went to apologize to the monk. They apologized profusely and explained everything. They asked the monk if they could please have the young boy back to give to the girl who was now a married woman. The monk said "Okay." He told the boy the whole story, and sent him home with his mother.

That monk didn't need to forgive. Why? He never had hurt or resentment or any sense of injustice in the first place. He was at that highest level of *"no self and no enemy."*

That monk's type of detachment is not "escapism" like we find in the pop-psychology and self-help version of detachment. For this highest level of achievement you must grab God so tight, embrace God the One Power so absolutely, that only that highest energy makes sense. He had reached such a high level that he could look down and know: "Your idea of chastity, your idea of name and reputation, your moral issues, they are all meaningless to me. They don't make sense to me, because they are not real." When they said to him, "Shame on you," he did not know what that meant. He was so pure inside, he never acknowledged such fake ideas like shame.

He didn't say, "I told you so!" or "I raised this boy and now you owe me $1 million for my expenses and the defamation of my character and my temple!" He didn't pull out his sword and chase them away. He didn't quote scripture to them or list his good deeds to defend the honor of his religion. No. His attitude was at a higher level then our human level. This monk's attitude is more like, "I have the only big Diamond in the whole world, while you guys have nothing. I have it and know that it is so precious, so I hold on only to this."

This kind of story is like a barometer. It shows you how high your level is. In your life, if you actually meet somebody who is at this high level, you are blessed. If you can see no evil and no enemy in your life, there are two possibilities: either you are at a very low level, or you are at a very high level.

Before we can get to that high level, we have to start our practice from a lower level. First we learn how to bear suffering, have patience and tolerance, learn not to argue with people, learn how to forgive. We learn how to be "good monks."

Nothing Between You and God
There should be nothing between you and God. This is very hard to do. We can practice this but we should never claim that we have achieved this. Why? Because in any second you can be distracted. You need to keep humble and watchful, constantly returning your focus toward God.

That's one reason those old religions set aside a "Sabbath" or holy days for worshiping God. It was to remind you and give you a chance to concentrate only on God at least for one day. But one out of every seven days is not enough. We need to remember God every seven hours, every seven minutes, every seven seconds. That is very hard to do.

Nothing should come between you and God, but most people cannot make it. For example, if you worship family, you will become a slave. That's why those old societies pushed "family" and family values, because if you follow that, then you can easily be made into their slave. There's always more you can do for your family, and those fake systems will sell you a lot of ideas based on your fear for your family or your good intention to help your family. You can easily end up putting family before God.

That's why those religions had practices like bringing the family together before mealtime to pray, blessing babies and marriages, and other family oriented rituals. You were supposed to remember to put God first, even before your family.

It can be very easy to forget God. We habitually reverse the proper sequence of things. If I worship money, that means I place money in front of everything. Then there's no room for God. I can worship fame, titles, a big house, my health, etc. Even when I'm hungry, I think of food first and forget about God.

Luxury and enjoyment are not bad, but they can become a problem because you can easily slip and start looking for security, pleasure and comfort and place them in front of God.

Likewise, if you choose a life aimed at glory and personal achievement, then you can forget to be humble and rely only on God. "Glory" means to be recognized out there by all those in that bubble world who do not believe in God. Why do you want to win that sort of recognition?

But if I have a life of luxury or accomplishment, and if they are both secondary to God, then that's okay. I can own gold, securities, and rule a whole country, as long as I place God in front of everything else.

This sounds easy, but it's not! When you place God in front of everything else, everything else loses importance. You start to handle all of your affairs very differently. It becomes harder to stay in a position of luxury and achievement, because you are no longer focused on them in the same way as the rest of the world.

You don't have to be poor, but ask yourself, "Why do I want to have a wealthy and comfortable lifestyle?" That's a mistake to start with. A baby doesn't care about its lifestyle. Does a baby care if it's rich or poor? You have to write off that concern.

Any time we value something, we put something between ourselves and God. To be with God is the utmost luxury. Knowing this, there should be nothing that you value in life but God. When people care about something, they are attached to it. That something had better be God.

Wall Street hires greedy people who turn around and punish the greedy. When you really think about it, if you seek their services, it's most likely because you have a certain amount of greed. After all, you go to them when you have a surplus of money because you hope for an even bigger surplus of money. But if I have nothing between me and God, I don't care about gaining or losing money and I have no fear or greed. Then, whether I invest with Wall Street or not, they can't hurt me. That means I don't worship the wrong God.

Our whole society is constructed to work against you. It's constructed to put barriers between you and God. As we said before, the world is invested in you being very busy and having lots of trouble. Without you getting sick, the whole hospital industry would collapse. No accidents? Then there would be no insurance. There needs to be a lot of trouble to keep this economy going. They need to encourage greed to get people to consume.

That's why they build houses bigger and bigger, because then you need more furniture, more utilities, more taxes, more landscaping, more, more, and more. You have to work longer hours, fret more about your investments, so that in the end, you have no time left for God.

Ultimately, to break out of this trap and overcome these barriers between us and God, we have to do what Jesus says: "What belongs to Caesar goes to Caesar, what belongs to the Kingdom of God goes to the Kingdom of God."

People wonder if there is a short cut to God. There is. Live in truth. Be pure like a baby. Live with your true heart. Just by thinking truth, you are already taking a short cut. Another short cut is to surrender yourself totally to God. You can reach Tao today if you can sincerely and truly do that.

Surrendering totally to God is like this: If you sit there talking to me, I feel as though everything you say bypasses me and goes directly to God. Then I do not answer you, I allow God to give an answer to you. Yield yourself to God. If you connect to God, then when people insult you, they insult God. If they laugh at you for being so different, they laugh at God.

We have to give up those colorful things that distract us, so that we can see God. Lao Tzu says *"hunting and games madden the mind."* The powers in this world want to keep you too busy to connect. They'll entertain you, distract you, put demands and expectations on you. That pulls your mind further away from your Te. Their control of money works that way too. They flood the system with lots of money and prosperity, or they take it away and starve you. Either way, they keep you so busy that it drives you crazy.

Yes, this is an evil empire. But do you want to spend your energy fighting that empire on this human level? Or do you want to go to God? Go ahead and pay your taxes, don't expect anything back. Just let Caesar be Caesar. Open a checking account or whatever you need to do so you can buy groceries, not because you like their system, but because that's the way it is. Use their system, but don't let them use you! Don't get too involved and distracted so that you end up looking away from God.

Use their system but don't get eaten by their system. Don't try to terminate evil, virus, bacteria, diseases; just leave them alone. Keep them at bay and keep yourself apart enough to coexist with them without getting infected by all the illness around you. Scrounge together as much freedom within your life as you can to meditate and connect to God.

How to connect to God? We have to qualify ourselves. Not by knowledge, but by getting rid of a lot of junk and upgrading ourselves.

This is how they used to train in the old Taoist and Buddhist temples. When you entered the temple, you were stripped of every artificial thing. You left your family, your home, your business, your friends, your reputation. Shaving your head was a ceremony to show that you gave everything up. Those monks left everything behind. Could you leave behind your wealth, your mother, your jewelry, your concubines?

When you enter the temple you have nothing left, including your name. You give that up too. The Master uses his spiritual ability to look into your past and from what he sees, he gives you a new name. After you get your new name, you get a new start. It serves as a "stop point". Before that point, you were chasing the artificial things in this world. Now you are going for the real stuff.

It's often the case that the more achievement you have in the artificial world, the further from God you are. When you give up all that, you start from ground zero again and start to qualify yourself. You start to change. You improve your feeling, thinking, and everything about yourself.

That's why when they agreed to train you in the old days, they made you become nobody first. Today, there are two ways to do that. You can do it the physical way by pretending to give up stuff by giving things away. Or, you can do this through mental training. You can learn to realize that we do not own anything. We don't own our own body; we don't own our kids, our wife, objects, land, or our house. Even our Te belongs to God.

If I have the privilege to connect to God, I am not going to let any artificial thing come into play, like my own likes, dislikes, or attachments. It's like I am holding onto this wire that carries 10 million volts. If I want to hold onto that wire, I shouldn't have any dust or debris attached to me, nor should I be touching anything else that would ground me. If I touch anything else, I'll get zapped. If I'm selfish, if I care about food, money, sex, what people think of me, anything at all, it won't work. Only if I'm floating clear can I touch 10 million volts and be okay. But as soon as I touch something else, I blow up. You have to realize that the kingdom of Caesar and the kingdom of God can never mix at all. If you want to touch God's voltage, don't touch anything else.

There is a paper thin division between real stuff and fake stuff. In your heart, as soon as you bid on an artificial goal or make a bid for truth, you are on your way to either life or death. They are totally different paths going in totally different directions. You cannot do both at the same time. When you want to be with God, you defy everything on this planet. You defy everything "not God."

Lao Tzu describes what it's like to live with nothing between you and God. Let's go back to Chapter 20 of the *Tao Te Ching* again:

> *"Give up learning and become worry-free.*
> *Is there a difference between obey and command?*
> *Is there a difference between good and bad?*
> *I fear what everyone else fears:*
> *So long this has been such a pointless idea.*

I wonder when it will stop
Everyone else is indulging themselves,
as if enjoying the sacrificial feast of the ox.
As if in spring some enjoy climbing the terrace at the park.
I alone seem unaffected and lost,
Like an innocent baby that hasn't yet learned to smile.
I alone have no place to go.
Others have more than enough,
but I alone am lacking.
I feel like a fool: as if I were confounded.
Everyone else appears bright,
but I alone am dim.
Everyone else appears to be so smart,
but I am the only one who is confused.
I like to be as unpredictable as the immense ocean,
as unstable as the gusty wind.
Everyone else acts capable,
but I'm the only one who acts stubborn and foolish.
I am different, but I am nourished by the great mother."
            Lao Tzu, *Tao Te Ching,* Chapter 20

Pay attention to where he uses the phrase "I alone." In order to connect, you are alone. You are not connected to what everyone else is chasing.

He feels "confused." Confused means he's sorting through everything that doesn't match that real truth. "Not this, not this, not this, not this, not this....." What is accepted as real in this world is unreal and confusing to him.

Lao Tzu says, "Everyone appears bright." Everyone in our world likes to boast "I know about this topic!" But Lao Tzu knows that this type of knowledge is nonsense.

"I feel like a fool!" he says. If you don't feel like a fool on this path and instead feel like an expert, something is wrong! Lao Tzu feels like a fool, like the only one. That means if you look around and you see that everyone is pretty much like you, then you are probably going the wrong way.

The energy of God is so hidden, so subtle, so refined and "small," it's like emptiness. If you want to hear that small little speck in the corner of the room, you better be so very quiet. That's why we have to get rid of everything just to hear life energy — it's so subtle. Between God and me, let there be nothing!

PART FIVE:
The Grand Tao

道

Restoring Ourselves – Restoring the World
We all have a span of time allotted to us within which we must burn off enough negativity, scrape away enough insulation, so that we can slip through and connect to that one pure signal of God. That is the purpose of this life.

We are given a limited span of time – one lifetime – in which to accomplish our goal. The first decade or two, most of us spend our lives enjoying the folly and enduring the hard lessons of youth. The next decade or two are usually consumed with making money, establishing a home, family and career, and all the routine cares of life. Before we know it, we are old. In old age we are wiser and realize that we really need to find a way to protect and develop our life energy. But suddenly we don't have the health and stamina we need to go out and find somebody to tell us *"how to,"* much less to practice. That's why every minute counts. When you are young and stupid, karma is chewing on you, but you have time to waste. When you are 30 or 40 years old, it's time to wake up and really hammer this out. If you are older, every second counts.

Whatever age you are, today is the day in that limited span of your life that you have landed on the real teaching. This is the way that will show you how to truly develop and use your Chi, how to clean and purify your life energy, how to clean and charge up yourself so that you can broadcast and receive a signal to and from God. This is an important point in your life, and what you do with this opportunity is pivotal.

There is great urgency for us to connect to God's power. The only way to make progress is by bringing back true sincerity. We can choose to live in a very naïve way in our nice house with a picket fence, eat nice food, raise a family, seeking new pleasures and approval all our life. But going down that same old road, rich or poor, everybody perishes.

Instead, we can use this time to beef up our original spiritual purity and strength. Remember, this human dimension is unique. It is only here where you have all the tools you need to repair and restore your life energy. You have Chi and Te together and can learn to access both. If you use this time to merely enjoy life as if it were a big party, you will lose this opportunity.

Jesus says enough faith can move mountains. That means if you are so truthful, so close to the origin of God, then you can connect with the same power that decreed: "Let there be light." Get closer to this power! That's what Jesus tried to teach. "The kingdom of God is within you….greater things than these shall you do!"

But restoring yourself is only part of the goal. If you can be so pure that you are able to pray for yourself, this is called "Small Tao." If you can connect and pray for the world, that is called "Grand Tao."

The true and serious goal of this book is to share this truth of the way of God with others. The impact of this teaching will be far and wide. Why? As more and more individuals learn how to transform themselves and become living connections with the Tao, they will increasingly bring that original plan of harmony and restoration not only into their own lives, but they will bring that signal of Tao into the whole world.

If we can raise our own energy frequency, that helps to raise the frequency of humankind and this world higher and higher, and perhaps raise it enough to correct the disastrous course our world is now on.

Let's go back to our cell phone analogy once again. Let's say I have a special cell phone that can reach everybody, everywhere at the same time. If I can touch that cell phone network and reach everybody at the same time, that means I can send out the same message to everybody, everywhere at the same time. I can broadcast whatever message I want, and everyone will hear it. That's what it is like to connect with the super-mainframe of universal energy. If I broadcast a message through the universal energy of Tao, the entire network picks it up.

If an individual has the power to connect to Tao, to listen to Tao, to broadcast to Tao, they also have the power to broadcast the energy of Tao out to the entire world. When the strong signal of original energy is broadcast into the world, there is a greater chance for our world to turn back toward the path of harmony and balance.

To do this, we must be able to both listen clearly and broadcast clearly. The book *T'ai Chi Classics* mentions these two fundamental powers of Taichi – listening power and broadcasting power.

Martial artists interpret that power to mean becoming sensitive enough to "listen" to what their opponent will do next. Those martial artists also work hard to "broadcast" an energy message to unbalance or control their opponent. A pinnacle achievement for a Taichi martial artist is the ability to "transfer power." With such ability, they can send out a powerful energy signal using little or no physical force and totally uproot and displace their opponent.

Actually, these powers that the *T'ai Chi Classics* talk about have less to do with martial arts and far more to do with spiritual ability. What we are really trying to achieve is the ability to connect to our Te so that we can "listen" to God and then "broadcast" that message into the world. In fact, at its root, listening power and broadcasting power are the two most fundamental powers of Taichi. You do not need anything else to become a master of Taichi.

As a Tao master and master of Taichi, I am not just here to teach people how to "transfer power" in the sense of throwing somebody through a wall. I am here to teach people how to transfer the power of God into the world.

If we are to reach this ultimate goal of Taichi, we have a lot of work to do. Only the real and true Taichi tradition preserves the training to both purify and strengthen our life energy enough to develop this real listening and broadcasting power.

The ability to broadcast that power of God is what Lao Tzu refers to when he says, *"The saint accomplishes everything through non-action."* It isn't that the saint sits passively doing nothing. It means that the saint doesn't take conventional action in this material world when he wishes to accomplish his goal. Instead, he connects to God and broadcasts that power and that signal out across that network. It is that power and signal which accomplishes his task for him. That is the true meaning of *"non-action's action."*

The old Buddhist teachings talked about working on the three vehicles. In Tao teachings, they talk about building a raft – either a small raft or a big raft. These vehicles and rafts were just symbols. They meant, "Can you build yourself a way to travel back to God?"

When you work on a small raft, or a small vehicle, that means you are practicing to restore your own personal connection to God. When you build a small raft, you can sail across the sea of limitation and death and arrive on the opposite shore of that higher dimension of God.

However, when you are working to build a great vehicle, or a big raft, that means you practice not only to restore your own connection to God, but to also have the ability to become like a broadcasting tower. You can send that message and power of God out into the world. Ultimately, you can use that big raft to help others reconnect with God.

The message in this book is reaching out to all of those who want to build themselves a small raft. It can help you fill all of those cavities inside, repair your life energy, plug you back into that network of God and restore your True Self. But this message is also for those who feel that call inside to build a big raft, and learn to transmit the powerful, nourishing and balancing energy of God out to this whole world.

The Rule of Balance

The essence of the One Power of the universe has a purpose and intention to keep going forever and to be in balance. In order to maintain that balance, there's both construction and destruction.

When we see the universe, we tend to see the constructive part. We don't normally see the destructive part. It's like when we drive through a city, we see the buildings, the bustle, and the glamour. We don't see the sewage system, the underbelly, the garbage hauled away at dawn, the demolition and decay.

Our human race has been humming along, consuming all the resources on our planet, abusing each other, abusing nature, using our power of construction to build our glamorous human civilization. We look at our short history and it appears we have endured many ups and downs and have somehow survived. It's as if a big dome protects the survival of the human race. But I worry that we will poke a hole in that dome. We can poke through that dome of protection when enough of us collectively broadcast a frequency of wrong thinking.

There is a rule to the Way of God, and the rule is balance. The rule is absolute. Since you have a piece of God trapped inside you, you have a piece of that rule inside you too. If you are humming a bad, destructive, distracting, artificial or "evil" idea, it overwhelms the signal of God's nourishing energy. Your mind becomes off-balance. That's why Lao Tzu says, "*Games and hunting drive your mind wild.*"

Selfish, artificial and evil thinking is anti-God's frequency. When we exercise our mind in a way that's "too much" or "too little" and become imbalanced, the only way to rebalance ourselves is to hook back into God's will so that God's nourishing signal can bring us back into balance. But the problem is that we don't do that. When we start to get out of balance, we reach for even more artificial and drastic human measures that finally tip us over altogether.

This rule of balance also affects us collectively. We are the tail-end of God. We all have a piece of original energy inside of us. That energy can help us and hurt us. It can hurt us because what we think and do registers on that network of Tao. As weak as it is, our thinking links up with God's frequency. As individuals, the scale of power of our thinking is so miniscule, it is irrelevant. But if we collectively all think the wrong idea, then it gets strong enough to touch that Net.

If I'm the only bad person vibrating a bad idea, that's no big deal. But when I have followers, and more people start to echo my bad idea of greed, selfishness and evil, then that bad signal becomes very loud.

Right now we have millions of people vibrating greed, selfishness, lies, evil and hatred for each other. If we all start thinking so crooked, and this crooked frequency starts to accumulate, it registers in a big way. When billions of people are all "vibrating" that same wrong out-of-balance note, it will be loud enough to conflict with God's energy frequency of nourishing, balance and harmony. If it gets irritating enough, God's energy immediately reacts — like when I accidentally sniff black pepper and sneeze. Watch out!

We have worshiped idols, rocks, even the sun in the past. Nowadays it's money, fame and power. When a large number of us collectively stop looking toward God and instead expect that a fake leader or a political party or some new technology is going to lead our world out of its mess, we are in trouble. We now have a critical mass of people worshipping those false gods.

We amplify this "noise" all the time. In our human world, when we want to motivate people to do things, we encourage them by using wrong ideas such as greed, glory or false purpose. These bad ideas spread like a virus by way of our globalized commercialism and technology. As the population increases, the number of minds echoing this contamination increases and the quality of the whole system goes down. You can see this as we choose to glamorize sin, success, money, fame, exploitation, meanness, waste, selfishness and unfairness. It's as if our world message has become "worship my sin."

That wrong note reaches that Net and will bring up a need for balance — a correction. As soon as that correction happens in God's mind, it instantly affects everything. There will be a "jerk" or "pop" as it were. The question is, "Can we survive it?"

Let's say we have both bad thinking and original thinking. These two can be a little bit imbalanced, say 60/40 or 45/55, and our world can keep going along with business as usual. But one day when good energy shrinks down to 20 or 30 percent, and the bad thinking raises to 70 or 80 percent, we are so off-balance that God is going to startle and wake up and say "enough!" That energy of the universe reacts instantly to erase that wrong thinking, because it is God's nature to maintain balance.

God's frequency is above that of our material world. Our material world is riding on top of this non-material force. So if there is the slightest change in that non-material force, that whole material world will shift automatically.

It's as if the whole universe revolves around the Center of God like a wheel. When that small center of the hub turns, the entire wheel automatically turns, no matter how large it is. If you are riding on that wheel, when that hub turns, you will turn too. But if you are closer to that hub, that turn is less disruptive. You'll only move a little bit. If you sit very far away from that hub's center, when it turns, you will have a much bigger revolution.

Hoping that human civilization will improve on its own is not very promising. The pattern of our history is build-up, collapse, build up, collapse. "Doomsday" is more like a cycle. It is a natural force of rebalancing. Our world has seen many disasters before. Many civilizations rise and fall, and these "doomsdays" are going to happen again.

But instead of working to soften the blow or avoid calamity by striving to restore balance and the natural way of God, we look away and distract ourselves with our busy human lives. Everybody prefers to live as if things will go on as they have before and they continue to conduct their business as usual.

Business as usual is very risky now. In the recent 100 years, we've very suddenly increased our population, and exponentially increased our reliance on our own rational thinking and technology. More distant from the natural way means we are heavier and further away from Tao. But if our frequency stretches so far away from the Center of that Net toward the outer limits of fake values and wrong thinking, it is like a strained rubber band. It stretches so far that it creates tension in the whole band and will sooner or later snap back very suddenly. We are so far away that it will be easier to "snap" back like a rubber band with great disruption.

People reading this may see a punishing God in these words. But that's not true. God's energy is not "good" or "bad," it's just there, everywhere, working toward balance. And no matter how far we try to run, sooner or later God's force of nourishing, balance and harmony will always prevail. The world will be "balanced," whether we like it or not.

The story of Noah's Ark is symbolic. The Noah scenario is this: Those who are very sincere and connect to that frequency of God will be protected. The water means God's power. The boat is that bubble of protection. They float around on that power, just like that boat washed here and there and finally ended up on dry land.

If enough people repent and get together and meditate to connect with God, then they can be in a situation where they can survive. They can benefit from matching their frequency close enough to the frequency of Tao so that they operate in a "bubble of protection." They escape that "judgment" when God rebalances.

You don't have to be 100% clean. If you were, you'd already be out of this dimension. We have to let the unrealistic idea go that we have to be totally pure in order to live right, to live with the true feeling of our Te. Human nature is human nature. We have sin and we have Te. We have both. But we have to manage and balance these two inside of us. We have to constantly work to clean ourselves up.

People worry about the end of the world. Don't worry about the end of the world. Rather, worry whether you have balanced yourself enough to be close enough to God's frequency so that you have that bubble of protection. When you don't have that bubble you are doomed to perish.

Our human civilization at this time has many serious troubles. It may not be possible to balance ourselves enough to prevent disaster. However, the message of hope in this book is that if enough people do whatever is necessary to restore their connection to God, we can broadcast a message, that signal of original energy, out into the world. That signal may change our world's course by an inch, or even a half an inch. But that may be just enough to correct our course so that more of us can survive when the rule of balance causes that "snap."

When we broadcast God's message of nourishing and balance across that Net to the entire world, the entire world will pick it up. Everybody has a piece of that Net inside of them. And even if it is buried under layers of insulation, contamination and even evil, our broadcast can raise that volume of God's message just enough that others will pick it up a little more clearly than before. If everyone on this planet picked up that original signal just a little more clearly, that may be just enough to keep us on a more stable track.

When a group of individuals who have restored their connection to God get together and "pray," that true signal can become very powerful and strong. Such a pure group's signal can go out across that network and have profound affect. That strong, pure signal beaming out from a circle of Tao masters can vibrate high enough to approach that power of "Let there be Light!" Even though they practice "non-action" they transmit the most powerful energy in the universe. Their combined meditation has the potential to change and heal our world by broadcasting outward the direct power and force of God. That's why in the temples of old they had Tao circles, where masters joined together to meditate and combine their energy into a very strong and penetrating frequency. They provided a beacon for that signal of God to beam out into the world.

But as we know, those old temples and real masters with such abilities have almost completely died out. We need to train up masters once again who have the dedication and calling to devote themselves to regaining this ability. We need to find people to whom this message, this teaching makes sense.

Take this book and give it to all the people you know who may be ready for this message. Start your own moving meditation practice, and learn the right way to feel and flow your energy so you can begin the journey back to Te. Don't waste a moment, and never give up. You have not found this teaching by accident. Just to find such truth is a blessing. This blessing means that this goal is real and attainable in this lifetime for you!

There is a resurging interest in spiritual matters today. And because the market demands it, there are now thousands of so-called "teachers" and religions and seminars and books bidding for your money, claiming they have some way to help you find your answers. But why wander around to so many new and untried teachings just because they sound pleasant to your ear? What good are they in the end if they cannot help you resolve the critical issue of life energy and connecting to God?

Those before us on this path of Tao wisdom have dug a tunnel through that mountain that goes 1,000 miles and comes out to light at the other end. We can use their tunnel, follow their footprints, and get a head start. Why start to dig your own tunnel from scratch or follow those who are just starting to dig? Time is short and the goal is critical. Choose your path very wisely.

Jesus talks about a man who finds a pearl of great value. He goes and sells all he owns so that he can buy that pearl. That pearl is like that diamond in Buddha's teaching. It is that precious piece of Tao, that kingdom of God inside you. Just like that man in Jesus' parable, now that you know what that jewel is and where that jewel is buried, you must do everything in your power to obtain it.

Not everyone can appreciate the value of this teaching. Some people may have quit reading this book many pages ago. That's normal. That's why Lao Tzu says:

> "The top wise men hear of the Tao
> and practice it diligently.
> Average intellects hear of the Tao
> and think about it once in awhile.

*Lower than average people hear of the
Tao and laugh out loud."*
>Lao Tzu, *Tao Te Ching*, Chapter 41

A wise person can look around and easily see that we human beings have tried our own tired, artificial, partial and limited solutions long enough. They can see that such solutions don't work in the long run, either for our own lives, or in our world. They never will, because they are solutions that separate us from God instead of bringing us closer.

Lao Tzu sent out an invitation with his words over 2500 years ago. I'm simply here to help that invitation be heard once again. The invitation is this: Let's go back and try another way. Let's try the original way we were designed to be. Let's try restoring that oneness with God, and let that power of Tao be the solution to our every problem. Let's rediscover Tao, the Way of God.

About the Author

From the age of twelve, Waysun Liao studied with a wandering Taoist and in a Taoist temple until he became a full Taichi and Tao master. Considered one of the world's foremost authorities on traditional Taoist wisdom and Chi arts, he is the founder and master of one of the oldest Taichi centers in North America, which is located in Oak Park, Illinois. He is one of the few remaining Tao masters carrying and transmitting the ancient oral traditions concerning the power of Tao, and shares his wisdom with students across the world.

Master Liao is the author of several books, including *Nine Nights with the Taoist Master*, *Chi: Discovering Your Life Energy*, and the acclaimed *T'ai Chi Classics*, which has been translated into nine languages. In addition, he has compiled a complete Taichi learning system on DVD, preserving the ancient temple teachings on moving meditation, the Tao, and internal energy development.

The website, *www.taichitaocenter.com*, is a primary resource for educational materials in the Tao wisdom tradition, including books, DVDs, and a schedule of Master Liao's training seminars and classes.

More from Master Waysun Liao

Chi: Discovering Your Life Energy

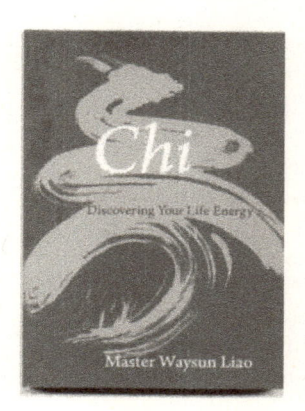

Here is a perfect introduction to Chi, the invisible energy of life that flows in and throughout us and the universe. Master Liao explains in a direct and simple way what Chi is and why it is essential to a healthy and vital life. Learn to recognize, develop, and strengthen your own Chi through specific breathing techniques and moving meditation forms. Published by Shambhala Publications.

T'ai Chi Classics

Master Liao translates three core classics of Taichi by ancient masters that comprise the "Taichi Bible." The full commentary illumines the texts' true meaning, and helps readers augment their experience of energy in Taichi. Illustrated with line drawings of the entire Long Form, the book also covers a basic history of Taichi and advanced applications of Jing energy. Translated into nine languages worldwide, and published by Shambhala Publications.

Nine Nights with the Taoist Master

Travel with Lao Tzu in this exciting novel that includes a powerful new translation of the Tao Te Ching. Lao Tzu travels to a turbulent border city in ancient China. At the prince's invitation, the sage spends nine colorful nights with scholars, traders, courtiers and monks explaining the power of Tao. Through this engaging story, Master Liao breaks the secret code of the Tao Te Ching, offering its life-changing teachings of mysticism.

The Essence of T'ai Chi

A pocket size abridged version of the T'ai Chi Classics. The Essence of T'ai Chi makes a great gift for new Taichi students. For experienced students, this book is a handy resource. Each paragraph can serve as a practice tip or meditation focus for your daily Taichi practice. Published by Shambhala Publications.

DVDs by Master Liao

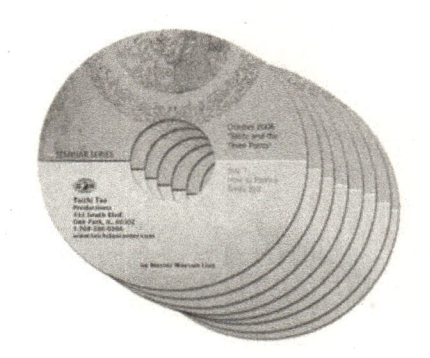

Enjoy live recorded classes and one-on-one teaching from Master Waysun Liao preserved in DVD format. You'll play these lessons over and over, learning key Taichi practice forms and meditation principles. Master Liao's DVDs offer a virtual temple where you can access the most traditional and powerful Taichi training style that was preserved for centuries in the Tao temples of China.

For more information about classes and seminars by Master Waysun Liao, or to order books, DVDs, and more, visit:

www.taichitaocenter.com

Printed in August 2023
by Rotomail Italia S.p.A., Vignate (MI) - Italy